The Administrative Career

The Administrative Career

A Casebook on Entry, Equity, and Endurance

Catherine Marshall
Katherine L. Kasten

CORWIN PRESS, INC.
A Sage Publications Company
Thousand Oaks, California

Copyright ©1994 by Corwin Press, Inc.

All rights reserved. No part of this book may be reproduced or utilized in any form or by any means, electronic or mechanical, including photocopying, recording, or by any information storage and retrieval system, without permission in writing from the publisher.

For information address:

Corwin Press, Inc.
A Sage Publications Company
2455 Teller Road
Thousand Oaks, California 91320

SAGE Publications Ltd.
6 Bonhill Street
London EC2A 4PU
United Kingdom

SAGE Publications India Pvt. Ltd.
M-32 Market
Greater Kailash I
New Delhi 110 048 India

Library of Congress Cataloging-in-Publication Data

Marshall, Catherine.
    The administrative career : a casebook on entry, equity, and endurance / Catherine Marshall, Katherine L. Kasten.
      p.   cm.
    Includes bibliographical references (pp. 131-140).
    ISBN 0-8039-6088-3 — ISBN 0-8039-6089-1 (pbk.)
    1. School administrators—United States. 2. School management and organization—United States. 3. Educational equalization—United States. 4. School administrators—United States—Case studies. 5. School management and organization—United States—Case studies. 6. Educational equalization— United States—Case studies.
    I. Kasten, Katherine L. II. Title.
LB1775.2.M27   1994
371.2'.01'0973—dc20   94-30530

This book is printed on acid-free paper that meets Environmental Protection Agency standards for recycled paper.

94 95 96 97 98 10 9 8 7 6 5 4 3 2 1

Corwin Press Production Editor: Marie Louise Penchoen

Contents

Preface   vii
About the Authors   x
Dedication   xii

1   The Professional Career   1
    Career Decision Making   2
    The Culture of the Profession   9
    The Rules of Assumptive Worlds   13
    Problematic Issues   16
    The Special Case of Equity   17
    Persisting and Enduring in the Profession   19
    Conclusion   21
    Recommended Reading   22

2   Examining the Issues Through the Study of Cases   24
    A Procedure for Case Analysis   27
    Conclusion   31

3   Entry Into School Leadership   32
    Case Studies of Entry Into Leadership   32
    Reflecting on Issues of Entry: Questions and
    Considerations   58

4   Equity Issues in School Leadership   66
    Case Studies of Equity Issues   66
    Reflecting on Issues of Equity: Questions and
    Considerations   92

5	Endurance in School Leadership	102
	Case Studies of Endurance in School Leadership	102
	Reflections on Issues of Endurance: Questions and Considerations	124
	References	131

Preface

Take your choice: Educational administration is either in the midst of exciting challenges, with new models for leadership and new policies supporting inclusion of teachers in decision making and inclusion of women and minorities, *or* the field is in turmoil, stress, and decline. Actually, both descriptions capture some truth about the field. We wrote this book to help educational administrators develop the skills and the habits for facing the challenges in our field. The case method of teaching, guided by insightful instructors, provides a popular, accessible means for discussion of critical issues in administration. We believe the case method, used with groups of educators, will help build professional norms supporting thoughtful and open discussion. Our book directs the discussion to cases of entry, equity, and endurance dilemmas.

Our special intentions are revealed in the book title. The book focuses on the dilemmas faced by those entering and shaping their career directions, on an array of equity issues, and on the issues that make it difficult to stay with the career—entry, equity, and endurance.

Although we have common career experiences, this book is our first collaboration, combining and, we hope, multiplying our strengths. The book capitalizes on our experiences working in schools and consulting with school practitioners and on our combined 24 years of experience teaching master's and doctoral students in educational administration.

Catherine Marshall has conducted research on the professional culture of school administration for 15 years, looking at values, norms, and language, as well as raising questions about the political nature of administration. Her particular focus has been on the struggles of administrators who take risks (atypicals), women and minorities, and on the special roles of assistant principals. These research projects were the basis for many of the book's cases.

Katherine Kasten's extensive experience with the case method and her research on school administrators' values and modes of action provided the grounding for fine-tuning our book for practical use in the classroom. As an administrator herself, she has experienced many of the tensions and dilemmas described in this book.

We can give only a generalized acknowledgment to our hundreds of students (at five different universities over the years) who have told war stories in response to our lectures on theory. Not only have they provided a refreshing sense of work life in schools but they have also reminded us of the power in connecting book learning to the complexities and perplexities of experience. Also, we are greatly indebted to those administrators and teachers who allowed us to interview them, to follow them through hallways, to read their outraged memos, and to listen to their private musings about the dilemmas they face. Although we have taken authors' liberties and disguised times, places, and names, we are in debt to them for this book's authenticity.

Finally, several people assisted with writing and editing cases. We thank Marcia Huth, Janice Gritz, and Katherine Feurst at the University of North Carolina at Chapel Hill and Madelaine Cosgrove at the University of North Florida. Each has provided gentle reminders to their professors about how to make the cases most useful to graduate classes. Frank Linn, technical editor with Taylor Engineering in Jacksonville, Florida, provided editorial support. As a former student of educational leadership and an astute observer of life in schools and other organizations, he brings a unique perspective to editorial work.

Preface

To our educational administration readers: Take this book and use it to develop the skills and the determination to persevere in the career and to make schools dynamic, fair, and caring places for educators and for students.

CATHERINE MARSHALL
KATHERINE L. KASTEN

About the Authors

Catherine Marshall is Professor in the Department of Educational Leadership at the University of North Carolina at Chapel Hill. She received her Ph.D. from the University of California, Santa Barbara, and has been on the faculty at the University of Pennsylvania and at Vanderbilt. The ongoing goal of her teaching and research has been to use an interdisciplinary approach to analyze cultures—of schools, state policy systems, and especially the culture of the profession of school administration organizations. She has published extensively about politics of education, qualitative methodology, women's access to careers, the assistant principalship, and about the socialization, language, and values in educational administration. She is also author of *Culture and Education Policy in the American States, Designing Qualitative Research, The New Politics of Race and Gender,* and *The Assistant Principalship: Leadership Choices and Challenges.*

Katherine L. Kasten is Professor of Educational Leadership and Chair, Division of Educational Services and Research, at the University of North Florida. She received her Ph.D. from the University of Wisconsin-Madison and was previously a member of the faculty at the University of Nebraska-Omaha. Her commitment to the study of educational organizations began with her experience as a teacher and teacher-leader at the high school and junior high school levels in Wisconsin and Michigan. Her personal experience as a university administrator and her academic study of the administration of educational organizations both shaped her interest in stories of administrative work. Her areas of expertise include the ethical dimensions of leadership, case teaching, teacher work-life, administrative licensure, and research methodology. In addition to numerous articles, she is coauthor of *Educational Leadership: Case Studies for Reflective Practice* and *The Licensure of School Administrators: State Practices and Policy Issues*.

To our mothers,
Grace Terry Marshall and
Katherine Lewellan

1

The Professional Career

What kind of people become the administrators in our schools? What inspires and supports them as they consider entering that profession? What happens when they face some of the persistent dilemmas? What do they do about the unfairness in their profession? What can they do about political pressures and about the ways the system fails certain children and their families? What are the rewarding enticements and satisfactions in their career? How do new realities and new policy pressures affect their ability to persevere? What makes them consider leaving? What sustains them? How do they endure?

In this chapter, we introduce the study of professional socialization with a summary of what we know about the profession of school administration. We focus, in particular, on entry into the profession, the resources and guidelines people use as they persevere in the profession, and the pressures and conflicts they find in the working world of school leaders. Educators who decide to become assistant principals are just beginning to face administrative career issues. In their daily lives and in new decisions as they move up in the hierarchy, they will continue to make choices about the profession, their personal motivations, their values, their politics, and their goals.

Career Decision Making

Few 6-year-olds say, "When I grow up, I want to be a principal." Young people do decide to become teachers, however, and they usually do so with lofty motivations such as a desire to make a difference, a desire to help children, or a desire to do something meaningful. As teachers become accomplished in working with children, some consider moving into administration.

Anticipatory Socialization and GASing

In considering whether to aspire to school administration, aspirants intuitively look at the profession's signals, the career map, the district's and the community's expectations for school administrators, who gets in, what is required to get in, how administrators are regarded, and what they do. As they anticipate moving into administration during "anticipatory socialization" (Merton, 1964), aspirants "try on" administrator tasks and roles. For example, some take volunteer leadership positions in coaching or leading Rotary Club activities in the community or serving on a school site or districtwide committee, which gives them visibility and experience (Griffiths, Goldman, & McFarland, 1965).

Aspirants begin to look and talk like administrators. They are GASing—getting the attention of superiors, that is: doing the extra work and hanging around so they will be seen as having leadership potential. All of this is rather informal and ambiguous. Those who have informal and social affiliations through clubs, sports, churches, and common cultural groupings find making the transition to administration more enticing and easier (Marshall, 1992c).

The Career Map and the Hierarchy

Observant aspirants notice that mobility in the career means crossing *hierarchical boundaries* up career ladders; *inclusionary boundaries* from the periphery to the center of decision making; and *functional boundaries*, as in a shift from one function such as personnel to another such as staff development (Van Maanen & Schein, 1979). They notice that, in most districts, greater prestige, power, career mobility, and salary come to administrators in the larger schools and with the older students. They recognize the systems of status and rewards. They see opportunities. Quite likely, they also see lots of gray hair. The profession is in the midst of massive retirements. Thompson (1989) predicted that 40% of the school administrators in 1989 would be retired by 1995.

A national study of mobility routes (Gaertner, 1980) demonstrated a common recognition that coaching positions and the secondary assistant principalship were common entry positions from which men launched administrative careers that led to the superintendency. The same study showed the elementary principalship to be one that is unlikely to lead to the superintendency. Ortiz's (1982) study of career patterns of minority and female administrators demonstrated that minority administrators usually enter administrative careers by supervising large groups of minorities or programs especially designed around minority issues.

Each district has its own stated criteria and processes for selecting among candidates for positions. Large cities have their own tests and maintain lists of aspirants for administrative openings. Most often local educators are selected for entry-level positions (e.g., an assistant principalship or a small-school principalship).

When districts decide they want "a change agent" or "new blood" or someone with innovative ways to "stir things up," they often select an outsider, someone with more cosmopolitan than local reputation and connections. Whether cosmopolitan or local, top administrative positions have become tenuous. With pressures from community expectations, board politics, and the press to use the school to solve social problems, the superintendent's position is often a position with high turnover.

Aspirants viewing the overall career map in school administration see that the field is dominated by White males. In 1992, 94.4% of superintendents nationally were men, 95% of high school principals were White, and about 4% of superintendents were non-White. Among administrators, the middle school level had the highest representation of Black principals with 9.3% and of Hispanic principals with 2.1% (Bell & Chase, 1993). Given the proportion of White males in the profession, it is not surprising that most of the theoretical literature in the field was developed without considering racial and gender differences (Shakeshaft, 1989).

Finally, norms in the profession have developed around the life cycles of men and outdated assumptions about men's and women's roles in the family and in society (Bell & Chase, 1993; Bourne & Winkler, 1982). Norms requiring administrators to attend many evening events and to work 60-hour weeks assume that the administrators can separate their personal lives from their work lives and control the demands of both. Norms requiring youthful, strong, athletic presence for leadership and early entry into the career assume that childbearing and child rearing will not interfere with career progression. Such norms hinder women's access. Today, these norms do not work well for either men or women, given the economic and social forces that affect men's and women's roles (Bell & Chase, 1993; Bourne & Winkler, 1982).

Aspirants also see that the most powerful (and highest paid) position, the superintendency, is generally filled by people more attuned to managing district politics, the media, and budgetary and bureaucratic issues. Most often, the higher the position, the more tenuous the connections between the position's tasks and the instructional program, teachers, and students. Few teachers (16% according to a National Education Association [NEA] survey in 1986) view principals as good sources for assistance with the knowledge and skills for effective teaching. Staying in touch with teaching and children as an administrator carries little reward according to the career map. The principal of a small neighborhood school serving lower-grade elementary children is often highly involved in instructional issues, but such a position is low in prestige compared to that in a large high school.

The Professional Career

District personnel hold understandings (usually unstated) that certain positions are right for certain types of people. Some of the unstated understandings include the following:

1. Schools in certain neighborhoods should have principals with rather strict discipline and quick decision-making styles, to fit with prevailing neighborhood assumptions about tough and assertive leadership.
2. Schools with large minority populations should have minority administrators.
3. Race and gender should be balanced on the administrative team.
4. Administrative teams of three or more should have one female administrator.
5. Certain administrative posts (e.g., the secondary assistant principalship or specific principalships in a district) are good training and testing positions for placing aspirants and protégé(e)s who might be considered for higher positions.
6. Some positions are of high status, either because they are rather easy assignments or, more likely, because they often lead to good visibility and higher promotions.
7. Some positions are seen as career or, more negatively stated, dead-end positions where a person stays until retirement.
8. Minority administrators should administer schools, districts, and programs with large minority populations and concerns.
9. Women administrators should not be paired on an administrator team unless there is a strong male administrator on the team.

Few studies document these understandings, yet many district personnel assignments and many careers are directed by them.

No actual career map is laid out, but those entering the career have some sense of the lay of the land. As they struggle to balance family, personal, and special-training pressures, they consider whether or not the career seems enticing and rewarding enough to help them feel a sense of fit, comfort, and satisfaction to endure and succeed. They make difficult decisions about whether or not to seek upward mobility.

Sponsors, Mentors, and the "Tap on the Shoulder"

When a principal or superintendent says to a teacher, "You know, you'd make a good administrator—you ought to take some courses and think about moving up," this is the tap on the shoulder, a rather direct signal that this person should consider an administrative career. Educators who have been recognized as having potential for administration often find that the people who identified them become mentors who are willing to give career advice and "be there" when novices face dilemma-laden situations. Even better, some aspirants may find that they have sponsors—advocates who will seek out positions and push their candidacy for career advancement with introductions to influential members of the profession, complimentary referrals, and the like. Sponsor-protégé(e) relationships often have a "built-in replication formula" (Valverde, 1974), as sponsors are more likely to identify with and support protégé(e)s who are very much like themselves in values, gender, ethnicity, social and cultural backgrounds, and behaviors. Sponsorship is especially important because upward movement most often occurs through sponsor-protégé(e) relationships, not through contest mobility, where merit and achievement and hard work will win the contest for the better positions (Turner, 1960).

Role Models and Task Learning

Most administrators say that, no matter how many courses and workshops they attend, the real learning occurs on the job and in following the lead of role models. They often model themselves after the kind of leadership they see enacted by several people whose styles and skills seem effective and seem learnable or adaptable for them. Performing administrative tasks provides more than skill building; the novice also learns certain attitudes and values (Breer & Locke, 1965). As administrators manage scheduling, negotiations with teacher representatives, site-based management team meetings, coffees with members of the Parent-Teacher Association, and staff development sessions, they learn what to value and what works.

Administrators who have allies in their district glean insights, learn political strategies, and get insider information through the "administrative grapevine" (Licata & Hack, 1980). They also acquire ways of thinking about deeper issues. Embedded in all the formal and informal communications among administrators, between administrators and teachers, and with community members are ways of viewing and valuing teachers as well as the relative value of various methods for communicating, supervising, and evaluating. For example, scheduling practices are grounded in convictions about the philosophical purposes for grouping students and about the timing of learning.

Formal Entry Requirements

Entry into an administrative position usually requires completion of state certification requirements. Each state has its own criteria for certification. Almost all administrative certification requirements include some years as a teacher as well as some university course work in administration (Ashbaugh & Kasten, 1992; Burks, 1989). A master's degree in educational administration is a frequent certification requirement.

University programs share a number of similarities. Entrance standards for preservice training are generally minimal (Cooper & Boyd, 1987; Cornett, 1985). Programs in educational administration and programs in teacher education are usually separate, different, and in different academic departments. Course work in school administration often includes an introduction to management, school law, finance, and personnel, and perhaps courses on models of leadership or seminars on contemporary issues in education. Many master's and doctoral programs include internships, acknowledging the importance of integrating the theoretical development with practical realities. Practitioners often pursue their master's and doctoral degrees by taking one or two courses at a time, generally in the evenings. Because most educators earn their degrees while keeping full-time jobs, they are never fully immersed in formal university preparation programs. Doctoral programs are more likely to require some intense study through residency requirements.

The doctoral dissertation can be quite a stumbling block for the aspiring administrator. Trying to stay connected to the networks that open job opportunities, to have a family life, and to conduct original research is an unsurmountable hurdle for many educators. However, the educator who aspires to move into a top administrative position learns that the doctorate is considered a signal of commitment, a symbol of expertise, and a mark of status—a desirable commodity.

Universities, state boards and legislatures, and administrator associations have all been active during the past decade in attempts to reform administrator preparation. The approaches to reform vary. They include efforts such as those by the National Association of Secondary School Principals (NASSP) through its Assistant Principals Task Force and the NASSP Assessment Center; the National Association of Elementary School Principals (NAESP); and the various state and local principals' centers. Foundations and businesses, ranging from McDonald's Hamburgers to the Danforth Foundation, provide supports and rewards for those who improve the preparation of administrators. The National Policy Board for Educational Administration focused specifically on reform in administrator preparation, and the 1991 report on education by the National Governors' Association's Task Force on Leadership and Management, *Time for Results*, advocated an action agenda for preparing effective principals.

The University Council for Educational Administration (UCEA), a professional organization of university professors of educational administration, is also concerned about improving the knowledge base and the preparation of school leaders. Currently, the National Council for the Accreditation of Teacher Education (NCATE) is working with several organizations to develop curriculum guidelines for programs in educational administration. Participating organizations include UCEA,

NAESP, NASSP, and the National Council of Professors of Educational Administration (NCPEA).

The Culture of the Profession

Every profession has its own culture. Whether or not they know it, people who decide to become school administrators are deciding to enter a culture. They leave the teacher culture, separating from teaching friends and colleagues and letting go of the values, tasks, and routines of teachers. They seek acceptance and inclusion in a new circle of colleagues among administrators (Marshall, 1992b; Merton, 1964).

The profession transmits its culture in visible ways. Aspects of it can be seen in what leaders pay attention to, measure, and control, and how they react to critical incidents. Culture is evidenced in role modeling, teaching, and coaching; the criteria used to reward organizational members; and the criteria for recruitment, selection, promotion, and termination of employees (Reitzug, 1992; Schein, 1986). Aspirants carefully look at the tangible evidence that represents the profession.

Controls Over the Profession

Professions are created so that people with similar tasks and values can control their lives. Out of common understandings and needs, members develop the following markers of their own professions: (a) a stated knowledge base; (b) a code of ethics; (c) control over the criteria for entry and promotion in the profession, including control of credentialing; (d) control over the laws that govern their work; and (e) methods for managing attacks on, or challenges to, their legitimacy. They also develop theory, knowledge, principles, specific language, symbols, and tools that distinguish them from others. When we hear them talking and acting as professionals, we can usually tell a lawyer from a neurosurgeon and a symphony conductor from a school principal—they are finely tuned through socialization into their respective professions.

Professions (and organizations) socialize new members to accept their cultural values and beliefs. Traditionally, rites of passage induct new members into a profession, sometimes including isolation and toughness-testing experiences similar to those that medical interns go through. Humiliating, humbling, and hazing pull the recruit away from old ways and lead to questioning of prior beliefs and willingness to accept the new norms and values of the profession (Inkles, 1973; Pascale, 1985). Thus entrants into a profession are vulnerable, searching for new ways and the approval of established members; they gain acceptance by mimicking the values and behaviors of experienced professionals. Aspirants who sense that their entry and endurance is weak, questionable, and resisted (as with women, minorities, and change agents) may initially deny that resistance and work harder to look like they belong.

Socialization into school administration is less formal and codified than socialization into professions such as medicine and law. Greenfield (1985) asserted that socialization into school administration is informal, random, and variable. Socializing agents have great influence over the recruits who go through socialization processes individually. Novices need strong support as they divest themselves of old roles but have to perform "organizational scut-work" (Greenfield, 1985, p 22). Because they are so alone and dependent and are often assigned low-level tasks, novices develop an "administrative self" that is less leaderlike and more managerial, conservative, and custodial. As a result, their values and behaviors tend toward conformity and deference to influential others.

Professionals develop common language, values, and skills and build cohesion in the ranks in a common effort to control their destiny. Administrators develop jargon and insider jokes (Bredeson, 1985; Marshall, 1988) but, unlike other professions, school administrators have no particularly esoteric, exclusive language that sets them apart.

Much of the socialization into administration occurs during the assistant principalship, the usual entry-level position. Ironically, with the critical and strong forces at work shaping future leaders for education, few scholars and policymakers have focused on the assistant principalship (Greenfield, 1985; Marshall, 1985, 1992a; Marshall & Mitchell, 1990).

Values

The historical roots of the profession of school administration lie in the fields of business management and public administration in the early 20th century, when Americans glorified the model of the efficient manager who kept schooling separate from political matters (Callahan, 1962). The model implied that administrators should not have personal and philosophical values or political stances that interfered with their jobs of managing an efficient bureaucracy. That myth of the apolitical administrator lingers, but most practitioners and scholars are now recognizing that administration is highly political and that administration is highly value laden. Further, the moral mission of schooling includes "molding character, shaping attitudes, and producing a virtuous thoughtful person" (Cuban, 1988, p. xii). The school administrator manages the moral and value-laden aspects of schooling as well as the technical aspects of buses and budgets. As Sergiovanni (1991) says, "Every technical decision has moral implications" (p. 42). Some researchers (e.g., Kasten & Ashbaugh, 1991; Leithwood, 1992; Marshall, 1992b) have developed research agendas to identify administrator values.

A growing movement among scholars recognizes the need to assist administrators in the effort to set forth an articulated set of professional values or a platform on which they stand for their professional careers (Calabrese, 1988; Osterman & Kottkamp, 1993; Starratt, 1991). Several scholars assert that administrators' human qualities and their desire to maintain a kind of critical vigilance aimed at constantly seeking improvement for schooling would be ways to create a new model of administrator—the critical humanist leader (Foster, 1986; Giroux, 1992; Purpel, 1988). Although models are emerging in the literature and in administrative preparation programs, most administrators have been untouched by these new approaches and are left to find their own ways in the midst of value conflicts and ethical dilemmas.

The American Association of School Administrators (AASA) developed a code of ethics for school administrators (Kimbrough, 1985). The code offers guidelines for school administrators but is not a platform for practice. The guidelines are seldom specific enough for dealing with a particular dilemma. Typically, the school administrator works out a value system and means of managing dilemmas on the job.

Doing so can be tortuous. First, the education system is fraught with value conflicts. Short of religion, nothing is so imbued with values as education. In our multicultural and interdependent society, languages, lifestyles, philosophical goals for schooling, and views about child rearing are all inevitably in conflict. Second, school policies are the result of political, value-laden choices. Administrators' work is the implementation of those policies—but the policies are not necessarily the ones that parents, teachers, children, or administrators would want to implement. For example, state legislators' views about the best curriculum requirements may not fit with a Hispanic family's heritage. Testing practices may conflict with what a teacher knows to be best for a particular group of students.

The philosophical goals driving American public schools have shifted over time and often conflict with themselves. We have school policies aimed at achieving efficiency and accountability; for example, maximizing the number of students in classrooms. We have school policies aimed at achieving quality; for example, minimum curriculum standards. We have policies aimed at achieving equity; for example, special programs such as Head Start. We also have policies aimed at providing choice; for example, parental and teacher involvement in planning and student options (Marshall, 1991). These policies conflict with each other, but school administrators must find ways to make schools function smoothly in spite of that.

Finally, school policy-making does not emanate from the values and motivations of educators, whose desire is to help children develop—as articulated by Noddings (1992), a caring ethic. School policies and structures may, in fact, stifle the caring ethic (Marshall, Rogers, & Steele, 1993). As a consequence, administrators face situations where the values of efficiency, equity, quality, and choice are in conflict and the caring ethic is not seen as legitimate. The dilemmas that educators face daily can be traced back to these inherent and chronic value conflicts in schooling. Administrators must find ways to manage within this conflict-ridden context.

The Rules of Assumptive Worlds

Common understandings about the literature and principles guiding school administrators have developed from combining scholarly works with the lore and craft of practitioners. Traditionally, leadership theory and organizational theory, borrowed from business management and supplemented with American cultural myths about heroic military, business, and political leaders, have undergirded the formal and informal training of most school administrators (Anderson & Page, 1993; Mitchell, 1982). One assumption, for example, is that top-down decision making and communication through a chain of command and hierarchical control are good, efficient, bureaucratic management. A second is that the tasks for teaching and administering can and should be specified, supervised, and evaluated; doing so will result in efficiency and high productivity in schooling. Such thinking, borrowed from bureaucratic management, may not work well for something so amorphous as good teaching and may not work for an organization where those at the bottom of the hierarchy (teachers) feel they know the most about how to do the work (National Education Association [NEA], 1986). Thus administrators' espoused theories and the theories that guide their actions may be confused and inconsistent (Sergiovanni, 1991) as they search for the right action, the best policy, or the useful guideline.

Administrators need to operate differently but they may not know how. New roles, for example, managing teams of an array of professionals dealing with at-risk children, present unfamiliar challenges. The public and legislatures are challenging the efficacy of school management; scholars, feminists, and critical theorists are raising sharp criticisms of the theory and practice in administration (Boyd, 1983; Ferguson, 1984; Foster, 1986; Griffiths, 1979). As a result, the knowledge base in the profession of school administration is shifting and unclear. The profession lacks an agreed-on knowledge base, one marker of professional status. Instead, administrators wonder what models to use and what principles to follow.

With their expertise and legitimacy challenged and no clear sense of what is correct, professionals expend a great deal of energy searching for ways to take charge and appear in control. Whereas such "take-charge" actions look like leadership according to traditional models, satisfying some audiences, they look archaic to others who seek new kinds of leadership and organizational meaning. In truth, as school boards and legislatures tighten accountability mechanisms, superintendents and principals have decreasing degrees of discretion instead of control of their destinies. Further, collective bargaining agreements, policies for site-based decision making, and movements for teacher empowerment are changing the structures within which school administrators must operate, without offering guidance for the cultural alterations that would follow.

At the same time, despite reform rhetoric about empowerment and shared decision making, administrators have more discretion and power than those they work with daily. Their professional culture, along with the pressure to make lots of quick decisions, tends to maintain top-down and controlling models of administration. Thus the models and basic knowledge for guiding the profession provide little clear guidance.

Given the lack of clear guidance for action, new administrators face a culture shock on leaving teaching and entering the new culture of school administration. They see practices that seem stupid, inefficient, hurtful, dysfunctional, sexist, or racist. Worse, they see them while in the frenzy of learning new roles, while being watched closely for task performance, and while being assessed for loyalty to the profession. Those who respond by bringing attention to the problems are viewed as disloyal, troublemakers, or poor team players. Most who aspire for upward mobility and want to be seen as competent and included in the culture learn the unstated understandings in the profession—the assumptive worlds (Marshall & Mitchell, 1991). As they work in their school sites, administrators learn the following rules of assumptive worlds:

1. Limit risk taking to small and finite projects.
2. Make displays of commitment to the profession and sponsors.
3. Do not display divergent or challenging values.
4. Remake policy quietly as a street-level bureaucrat.
5. Keep disputes private.
6. Avoid moral dilemmas.
7. Avoid getting a troublemaker label.
8. Cover and guard all areas in your job description.
9. Build trust among the administrative team.

Accepting these assumptive understandings helps administrators work together and fit within the professional ethos more comfortably. Assumptive understandings also constrain administrators' initiative and help develop a restricted repertoire of acceptable values and behaviors.

Sponsors and mentors assist novice administrators in feeling comfortable and justified in adhering to these rules. In many instances, the recurrent dilemmas they face make the adoption of these rules the only way to get through the day! For example, faced with chronically inadequate resources, time, and personnel to meet the policy demands for special education students, site administrators with the responsibilities for keeping things running and getting needs met act as street-level bureaucrats, balancing official policies and procedures against the needs of the children and families they meet daily (Lipsky, 1980; Weatherly & Lipsky, 1977). Site administrators quietly create their own systems or practices so that things will work, whether or not they comply with policy.

Problematic Issues

This description of career decision making and the professional culture of school administration raises several problematic issues. Administrators must gain access and support and develop a professional identity for themselves while dealing with and managing the following complex and dilemma-laden issues:

1. The profession has entry processes that have built-in barriers to the access of women and minorities, although women are 70% of the teachers and reform rhetoric emphasizes the need for minority children to have role models.
2. The profession is in a continuing search to identify an agreed-on knowledge base—the requisite values, knowledge, and skills, and the "correct" model for school administration—while the dominant model of top-down technical management persists.
3. Nonpractitioners affect their work because local, state, and federal policymakers and university scholars have varying degrees of power over the profession through control of preparation programs, evaluation, and licensing.
4. With only abstract principles as guidance, administrators resort to the rules of assumptive worlds when they face situations laden with value conflicts and ethical dilemmas, which often repress and hide the conflicts, leaving the root problems unresolved.
5. Because administration and teaching are separate, although mutually dependent, cultures (Ortiz & Marshall, 1988), administrators separate themselves from teachers and students as they move up in the career mobility system and become more attuned to political and managerial aspects of schooling, often losing the understanding that comes from intimate involvement in the teaching-learning process.

6. Taking time for critical reflection, new learning, and advanced education is risky for several reasons. The culture rewards loyalty and shuns critics, the daily work pressures allow no time for contemplation, and those who take a year off (e.g., for doctoral work) may lose their career opportunity.
7. Socialization processes promote the development of risk-aversive, conformist administrators.
8. Policy directives from boards and legislatures may require administrators to work at cross-purposes, enforcing programs that conflict with each other or with the realities at their site, and they usually provide few or no new resources or discretion for good implementation.
9. School administrators' status, legitimacy, and respectability have declined, both from community challenges about effectiveness and also from policy directives for shared decision making, empowering teachers and parent advisory councils.

Administrators have to fashion an identity in a profession fraught with pressure and ambiguity while learning skills and attitudes on the job. Moreover, this transformation most often occurs in volatile, challenging situations with high visibility and responsibility. Nevertheless, many educators take on this challenge, believing that they can improve schooling and believing that the status, the salary, and the control in the administrative career will provide a good life. They learn to trust their own judgment and find good advice and support. They learn to assess their accomplishments and learn to make their careers manageable.

The Special Case of Equity

Today, the most popular value to promote in the culture of administrators, as seen in their talk and in policies and programs, is *quality* (Marshall, Mitchell, & Wirt, 1989). Current policies aimed at quality include those for raising curriculum requirements and testing standards, lengthening school days, and tightening accountability. Although *equity* was a dominant value in the policy agenda of the 1960s and 1970s, advocates for equity are more likely to be challengers, not insiders, in today's educational circles (Clark & Astuto, 1986; Marshall, 1991). Still, school administrators, especially those who remain close to the students and their families' and teachers' concerns, face pressing equity issues every minute of every day. They deal with poverty, minority groups, and multicultural issues; they deal with gender equity, with access for those with disabilities; they must take on health issues about which medical, religious, and family systems disagree. These issues range from adolescents' search for gender or ethnic identity and meaning to adolescent pregnancy, sex education, and AIDS prevention.

Sometimes administrators face situations that make them wonder whether the system they are supporting is really equitable. Idealistic educators derive excitement and heightened motivation when they know they are helping a child overcome learning disabilities or have the chance to go to college. However, when they have to enforce a rule that has the effect of cutting off opportunity or creativity in a teacher or a student or, to reduce conflict or increase efficiency, they have to repress or submerge someone's idea, expression, need, or energy, those idealists feel the systemic dilemmas.

Those who pause in their work to think about the fundamental purposes of schooling are forced to ask about the school system's role in perpetuating inequities. Disgruntled parents, students, and teachers raise questions. Administrators see the continuing disparities in opportunity and ultimate life outcomes between male and female students, between minority and majority students, between lower and higher socioeconomic students, and they wonder whether their schools are just sorting machines. When they find that they have to cut off services and ration resources, they question whether schools can be much more than warehouses for children, especially children with pressing needs. When they find themselves evaluating teachers in ways that reinforce teachers' attention to orderliness, time on task, and preparation for achievement, they wonder where schools make room for child development, nurturing, serendipity, spontaneity, creativity, and fun. When they find themselves catering to the demands of potential employers, corporate donors, and parent-teacher associations to raise funds, they have to wonder what richness and diversity of goals and perspectives are lost by such channeling.

Persisting and Enduring in the Profession

School administration is not easy. Although educators understand that higher pay, status, control, discretion, and power positions are found by moving up the administrative ladder, the aspirant must make tough choices. Job descriptions, expectations, and norms for administrators were developed around the assumption that White males would hold the top positions and that they would have homemaker wives who could handle the family life. School administration norms were established, too, when the public and policymakers gave more trust, legitimacy, and discretion to school administrators, and the values promulgated through school practices were not openly challenged (Tyack & Hansot, 1982). Times have changed, and these outdated and narrow norms need changing too.

With overt barriers to women and minorities obtaining better paying jobs, with women entering administration while still having to fulfill many of the traditional female roles, with more single parents, with gradual societal redefinitions of family roles, with wives needing and wanting to have careers, with husbands needing and wanting to have time with their families, school administrators find the norms requiring 60-hour work weeks untenable. Administrator stress has always been a problem; these recent developments, unaccompanied by role redefinitions, have made the stress intolerable at times. Strokes and deaths are the more dramatic results. The subtler outcomes are divorces, resignations, quieter illnesses like ulcers and alcoholism, and the uncounted numbers of educators who know they could be good leaders but eschew administrative careers to maintain a better quality of life.

Administration has few tangible outcomes. Administrators must have some degree of self-generated perseverance and persistence, some way to keep on believing. A painter can see the sparkle of fresh paint on a house, but administrators must live on a few "good job, Fred" comments and just believe that their intense planning and constant activity make a difference. This is particularly difficult in an era when schools are microcosms of difficult societal problems, are given fewer resources and discretion to accomplish the tasks, and are scrutinized suspiciously by constituent groups, including the media and politicians.

Finally, administrators' capacity to manage and endure is undermined when they honestly do not know what is right. With some policymakers promulgating teacher empowerment and others insisting, at the same time, that teachers must be tightly supervised, what should they do? With mentors and sponsors giving them advice about how to handle political conflict by managing information, co-optation, or repressing dissent, and others calling for relationships based on trust and openness, what should they do? Will old models work? Should they develop moral arguments and become critical humanist leaders, searching for ways to make schools more democratic, as some scholars advocate? Further, when they see the daily realities that remind them that schools are not set up to provide what children need, what is the right "leadership" act? Should they do the best they can to keep the system functioning, or should they start a campaign to call attention to the inefficiencies, the false assumptions, and the low political support, thus challenging the system that pays them? In the meantime, how should they help that pregnant girl, that stressed-out teacher? What can they do *today* about the high proportion of minority children in special education?

Administrators face persistent career dilemmas about enduring, believing, and working hard, even sacrificing their own interests. A teacher's complaint, a new and seemingly impossible demand from the legislature, a recurring argument at home—any *one* problem would be manageable in good times, with good support, workable guidelines, and high energy. But administrators with few supports and administrators with too many such problems cannot endure. By opening discussion, this book can help administrators discuss entry, equity, and endurance in their professional careers. It may provide the basis for training and ongoing support networks.

This book has three fundamental purposes: (a) to help aspirants to positions in educational leadership and those with experience in the field of administration examine the persistent dilemmas of the profession in an effort to develop common descriptions and understandings, (b) to develop and nurture in administrators the habit of critiquing the status quo in continual search for better schools, and (c) to assist in the development of a personal platform for professional practice (Osterman & Kottkamp, 1993; Sergiovanni & Starratt, 1983; Starratt, 1991). A platform might be a concrete, written statement that expresses what the professional feels is important to professional practice. More likely, however, the platform is composed of unwritten and unarticulated, but deeply held, values and commitments. In either form, a platform is an ethical gyroscope that guides professional actions and choices. The discussion in this chapter and the examination of the case studies in the chapters that follow will assist the professional in developing a personal platform for practice.

Conclusion

Those who enter the administrative career in education will need to confront some difficult professional challenges. This chapter has provided a framework from professional socialization theory and from research on educational administration. This framework can be used to expand and apply the cases, to formulate theoretical and practical arguments for transforming the profession, and to generate discussion about the fundamental purpose of educational administration. The following are recommended books related to the issues presented in chapter 1.

Recommended Reading

Blase, J. (Ed.). (1991). *The politics of life in schools*. Newbury Park, CA: Sage.

Blumberg, A. (1989). *School administration as craft*. Needham Heights, MA: Allyn & Bacon.

Burks, M. P. (1989). *Requirements for certification for elementary schools, secondary schools, and junior colleges* (53rd ed.). Chicago: University of Chicago Press.

Daresh, J. C., & Palyko, M. A. (1992). *The professional development of school administrators: Preservice, induction and inservice applications*. Needham Heights, MA: Allyn & Bacon.

Evers, C. W., & Lakomski, G. (1991). *Knowing educational administration*. New York: Pergamon.

Foster, W. (1989). Toward a critical practice of educational leadership. In J. Smyth (Ed.), *Critical perspectives on educational leadership* (pp. 39-62). New York: Falmer.

Hart, A. W. (1993). *Principal succession: Establishing leadership in schools*. Albany: SUNY Press.

Hodgkinson, C. (1991). *Educational leadership: The moral art*. Albany: SUNY Press.

Jentz, B. (1982). *Entry: The hiring, start-up and supervision of administrators*. New York: McGraw-Hill.

Marshall, C. (1992). *The assistant principal: Leadership choices and challenges*. Newbury Park, CA: Corwin.

Marshall, C. (1993). *The unsung role of the career assistant principal*. Washington, DC: National Association of Secondary School Principals.

Noddings, N. (1992). *The challenge to care in schools: An alternative approach to education*. New York: Teachers College Press.

Ortiz, F. I. (1982). *Career patterns in education: Women, men, and minorities in public school administration*. South Hadley, MA: J. F. Bergin.

Parkay, F. W., & Hall, G. E. (1992). *Becoming a principal: The challenges of beginning leadership.* Needham Heights, MA: Allyn & Bacon.

Sergiovanni, T. J. (1992). *Moral leadership: Getting to the heart of school improvement.* San Francisco: Jossey-Bass.

Shakeshaft, C. (1989). *Women in educational administration.* Newbury Park, CA: Corwin.

Wolcott, H. F. (1973). *The man in the principal's office: An ethnography.* New York: Holt, Rinehart & Winston.

2

Examining the Issues Through the Study of Cases

Case studies provide vicarious experience of the dilemmas and tensions that administrators face. The 33 cases in this book were developed from interviews with school administrators and are grounded firmly in day-to-day experiences in schools. They have been fictionalized to mask the identities of the people and school districts involved and to give them dramatic coherence, but they are, nevertheless, very real.

The case studies in this book are organized into three chapters arranged around the central issues of socialization in the profession of educational leadership. Chapter 3 includes 13 cases that focus on entry into the profession. The 10 cases in chapter 4 focus primarily on issues of equity, issues that are particularly troublesome to many educators. Chapter 5 includes 10 cases that focus on issues related to endurance in the profession.

Although the cases are organized into chapters following the parameters described, each case introduces many issues for discussion and analysis. Several of the issues that might be introduced in the discussion of each case are identified in Table 2.1. This matrix will help readers identify cases throughout the three case chapters that deal with similar issues.

Case Number and Name	Entry: Upward Mobility and Career	Entry: Meeting Criteria	Entry: Relations With Teachers	Entry and Equity: Values and Rules	Equity: Gender and Sexual Orientation	Equity: Special Needs	Equity: Race	Equity: Accountability	Endure: Balance and Stress	Endure: Taking a Stand	Endure: Politics and Ethics	Endure: Parents and Publics	Endure: Role Conflict	Endure: Student Issues	Endure: Personal Life
3.1. Could She?	X	X			X				X						
3.2. Whistle-Blowing	X			X											X
3.3. Overqualified	X	X			X					X	X				
3.4. Irresponsible Friend	X		X					X			X				
3.5. Special Education Transition	X	X			X	X									
3.6. Responding to the Tap	X	X			X		X								
3.7. Detentions for Bathroom	X		X	X	X			X							
3.8. You Can't Ask	X	X								X	X				X
3.9. Stultifying Reprimand	X					X		X			X		X		
3.10. Too Many Crises	X	X	X		X		X	X	X			X		X	X
3.11. Rules			X	X				X					X		
3.12. Firing Elderly Teacher	X		X					X		X					
3.13. "Ms. Goody-Goody"		X		X	X							X			
4.1. Equity, Access, and Assessment	X	X					X	X				X	X	X	
4.2. Peabody's Blue-Ribbon Task Force							X	X			X	X	X		

(Continued)

TABLE 2.1. (Continued)

Case Number and Name	Entry: Upward Mobility and Career	Entry: Meeting Criteria	Entry: Relations With Teachers	Entry and Equity: Values and Rules	Equity: Gender and Sexual Orientation	Equity: Special Needs	Equity: Race	Equity: Accountability	Endure: Balance and Stress	Endure: Taking a Stand	Endure: Politics and Ethics	Endure: Parents and Publics	Endure: Role Conflict	Endure: Student Issues	Endure: Personal Life
4.3. Cultural Diversity	X						X						X		
4.4. "Sticks and Stones"	X			X			X			X	X		X		X
4.5. Strength		X		X	X				X	X	X	X			X
4.6. Trusting	X	X					X			X	X				X
4.7. Humor of The Hambone				X	X			X		X				X	
4.8. Potty Duty			X			X		X			X				
4.9. Children at Risk						X			X					X	
4.10. Taking a Stand			X			X				X		X	X		
5.1. Success and Family	X	X							X						X
5.2. Require Too Much?									X						X
5.3. The Call	X						X			X	X		X		
5.4. Stretching Truth			X	X				X		X	X		X		
5.5. Concerned Parents			X					X		X	X	X	X		
5.6. How Far?						X						X	X	X	X
5.7. Guns		X		X	X		X		X			X		X	X
5.8. Punk Queen				X						X	X	X		X	
5.9. Retiring Superintendent			X								X		X		

Examining the Issues

The remainder of this chapter describes a four-step process for analyzing the cases that follow. Readers, course instructors, and seminar leaders who wish to follow a more informal approach to case discussion are referred to the "Questions and Considerations" section at the end of each chapter of cases. That section includes discussion questions and additional activities that may be used in conjunction with case discussions.

A Procedure for Case Analysis

Although life may sometimes imitate art, it rarely has the narrative structure of good stories. Case studies, even those solidly grounded in real events, have a logic and rationality that would be absent in real life. Nevertheless, the *first step* in case analysis is to make sense of an uncertain situation, to set the problem (Schön, 1983). We have provided a tentative frame of reference for these cases by placing each in a chapter with several other cases related to the same key issue: entry, equity, and endurance. Yet each case also raises several other issues. In the case matrix, several other issues related to each of the cases are identified. The reader may find, however, that yet another definition of the central problem seems more appropriate. In other words, we have provided our perspectives on the central problem in each case, but readers may define or describe the central problem differently. Personal experience will influence definitions of the central problem. Each statement of the central problem should be concise and defensible.

Theory and theoretical concepts and constructs are often helpful in framing the problem. The reader may find, for example, that the problem may be framed by contrasting open-systems and closed-systems perspectives (Owens, 1991), or by comparing Theory X and Theory Y assumptions about human motivation (McGregor, 1960). Theory and concepts related to professional socialization, as described in chapter 1, should be particularly helpful in analysis of these cases. In fact, case analysis provides one test of the heuristic value of theory as it is applied to the description of complex experiences.

Framing the central problem is never easy. It is made even more difficult by the fact that what the central character sees as troublesome and problematic and what the outside observer (in this case, the reader) sees as troublesome and problematic may not be the same. People who are well socialized in the profession may have easy solutions that novice administrators find appalling. Critics of schooling question the very structure and assumptions that helped create the dilemmas. Identification of a problem is a window to the values and commitments of the central character (Harrington & Garrison, 1992) and, at the same time, to the values and beliefs of the case analyst. Answering some questions is helpful.

- What assumptions did the central character make in framing the problem?
- Are these assumptions appropriate or, alternatively, problematic in themselves?
- What other perspectives and assumptions can the reader bring to the experience?
- How would school critics view this situation?

What one person sees as disconcerting or debilitating, another might view as filled with opportunity and possibility. What one person sees as intrusive administrative control, another might view as clear directives.

The *second step* in case analysis, then, is identifying the implicit assumptions of the central character. Assumptions may be defined as rules of thumb, commonsense beliefs, or conventional wisdom (Brookfield, 1992). The rules of assumptive worlds are, in fact, assumptions about what works in administrative practice. Assumptions about the nature of education and how people learn, about the qualities of good leadership, and about fundamental values are central to the practice of school administration. As Brookfield (1992) noted, they "frame how educators practice their craft" (p. 13). These assumptions may become more apparent when they are contrasted with other assumptions that might have been made.

Cases in the book are of two types: (a) those in which the main character has made a choice or decision and now has difficulty dealing with the consequences and (b) those in which the main character faces a difficult choice or decision. The first type of case asks the reader to judge a decision already made. The second asks the reader to make a decision or recommendation. The distinction is helpful. Analysis of both types of cases involves the delineation of options, either the options that were open to the central character at the time the decision was made or the options and choices the central character faces at the end of the case.

The *third step* in case analysis, then, is to identify the options. Cast a wide net and include creative options unconstrained by bureaucratic rules and political, practical, and fiscal limitations.

Finally, the case analyst should select a preferred option that identifies what actions the central character should take or what alternative actions the central characters should have taken. Here, the case analyst compares various options and selects the one that seems most appropriate given the situation. Again, the choice is not easy. Some options are more appropriately "care full" (Noddings, 1992). Some are more educative, that is, most likely to promote learning (Evers & Lakomski, 1991). Some are more consistent with important ethical concepts such as freedom of expression, personal liberty, due process, democratic processes (see Strike, Haller, & Soltis, 1988), and conceptions of fairness and justice. Different groups may benefit from different options, and choices must be made mindful of who stands to benefit from particular decisions (Foster, 1989).

Choices are easy when one option is clearly preferable. More commonly, however, no good option is available, and the choice must be made among various kinds of compromises. Just as the options central characters have already selected provide insights into their values and assumptions, the options the case analyst recommends reflect personal values and assumptions that are part of one's platform for professional practice.

Often, delineation of the options and selection of the preferred option are enhanced by dialogue. The conversation may be a private one in which the case analyst tests the choice against alternatives by comparing the advantages and disadvantages of different choices. Discussions with others are also helpful, as differing perspectives, differing sets of assumptions, and differing values and beliefs are applied to the case (Ashbaugh & Kasten, 1991). Analysis may be enhanced by discussion with people outside the profession of school administration as well.

Searching for options and choices and critiquing assumptions help administrators develop the habit of constantly searching for alternatives to improve schooling. Quick fixes and mechanical responses to problems produce only short-term relief. As the profession of educational administration develops, support and rewards for the efforts of individuals who question and critique the status quo will be increasingly important. Inviting the perspectives of those who challenge the ways schools work, even those who openly criticize educators or have dropped out of the system, is another way the profession can be strengthened.

In summary, formal case analysis includes four important steps:

1. State the central problem.
2. Identify important assumptions.
3. Identify options.
4. Select the preferred option and defend the choice.

For each step, case analysis also involves justification of the choices and decisions made through use of the facts presented in the case, theoretical frameworks that are applicable to the case, legal precedents and constraints, and reference to transcendent values and beliefs.

Conclusion

This book is an inquiry into issues of professional socialization carried out through reading the cases in the chapters that follow, analyzing the cases to unpack the issues, and discussing the cases and the analysis with others. Harrington and Garrison (1992) summarized the possibilities: "Cases provide opportunities for inquiry . . . bounded by experience, framed by theory, generating possibilities, and transforming practice" (p. 721).

We have provided the cases, the experiences of others who have confronted the dilemmas endemic in the professional world of school administrators as they entered the profession, encountered inequity, and endured in the face of tensions and conflicts. These experiences are richly heuristic. We have also provided the instruction to develop skills of critical self-reflection, the habit of constantly searching to find creative solutions to the recurring dilemmas of school administration, and an articulated platform for professional practice.

Theoretical considerations have been introduced in chapter 1 and may be expanded through examination of standard textbooks in the field and through formal university course work. This chapter has presented guidelines for using the cases for discussion of practical and theoretical issues in educational administration. The responsibilities for generating possibilities and transforming practice fall to the reader, as the issues introduced in this case book are described, discussed, analyzed, and refined with the intent of transforming the daily actions and ordinary practice of school administrators.

3

Entry Into School Leadership

The cases in this chapter concern issues of entry into school leadership—being recognized as having potential as an administrator, obtaining an entry-level position, making the break with teacher colleagues, and proving oneself in an administrative position.

Case Studies of Entry Into Leadership

3.1. Could She Turn It Down?

Yvonne Martinez's position in central office as an instructional supervisor had been very comfortable for the past 10 years, but now she felt that everything in her life was changing. She had to respond to the superintendent's persistent pressure for her to take the middle school assistant principalship. She was certainly tempted; the "reorganization" of central office would change her current position in unpredictable and scary ways. She and other central office personnel were worried and tense, and the superintendent was offering no reassurances that they would like the changes.

Several people wanted that assistant principalship position—but Yvonne was not sure she did. She had no clear reasons for turning down the chance. So, why hesitate? Maybe it was because the new principal was from out of state and unknown to her. Maybe it was because so many others (who would see themselves as better qualified and having paid more dues than she had) wanted the position. This particular middle school had a faculty who had resisted the middle school restructuring 2 years ago. The situation might be impossible. And after she had spent all these years working with teachers on curriculum development and coordination, she was not sure she could still be effective with early adolescents.

Yvonne felt a bit embarrassed about her fears and suspicions, but they were based on the political sense she had gleaned from years of watching administrators in school districts. Was the superintendent pushing her just so he would look good? This was a good possibility because the state's biggest district now faced a class action lawsuit alleging sex discrimination in administrative hiring. Yvonne's district had never employed any female administrators except in the smallest elementary schools. Rumblings began and gained momentum. Was her superintendent setting her up? If she said no, she might jeopardize her comfortable central office job. If she said no, others might see her response as proof that women just were not up to the demands of secondary administration.

Also, she had to consider her mom. For the past 6 months, her mother had experienced one crisis after another—sudden widowhood, large medical bills from her husband's illness and too little insurance, debilitating migraine headaches that made her very dependent on Yvonne. This was a bad time for a job change. Still, this was the opportunity for a line position that could lead to a principalship or higher, positions she thought she had always wanted. Besides, Yvonne had held back her aspirations so many years while helping her husband establish his career. Why should she have to hold back again because of family commitments? Yet these issues were too personal to discuss with the superintendent. He had said, "Talk it over with your husband and let me know in 3 days."

Her misgivings seemed trivial when she did talk them over with her husband, who was thrilled at her opportunity. She did not even know what questions to ask or what assurances to seek when she talked with the superintendent again.

3.2. Whistle-Blowing

As he saw it, this middle school assistant principalship was his third and probably last chance to become a school principal, and he—at age 40—was about to blow it again over an issue with a custodian. Tall, athletic, a "local boy," energetic, outgoing, and witty—Chester Randell had been a natural for an administrative career. In fact, in his early thirties he had been invited to participate in a federally funded project that ended up being *the program* because almost every participant catapulted into administration. He had been placed in a central office internship assisting with the district's federal projects. After that, he received a special assignment as interim principal of the district's alternative high school programs.

Patiently putting up with stupidity, waste, and inaction was not easy for Chester, even though he kept encountering situations that called for such patience. "If I gripe about something more than twice, then it's past time to act," Chester always said. "I'm like my daddy was; he never said much but you knew that whatever he felt strongly about, he'd act on it and watch out—get out of the way!" Chester had little patience for bureaucratic rules or slow deliberate group processes. He was a "jock"—equally comfortable on the basketball court, the golf course, or in the middle of the action of the middle school assistant principalship.

Chester's first lesson in real-world administration came during his central office internship when he discovered that the director, his boss, mismanaged funds. Chester recalled, "I collected documents and watched and got all of this to the superintendent and I was sure I was going to be a big hero. The superintendent praised me, saying this was the kind of action he needed to make ours a great district. But you know what? Nothing happened. The big guy took early retirement with a cushy golden parachute."

Assigning him to an interim principalship, the next superintendent told Chester he suspected illegalities in the alternate programs and wanted Chester to use his skills to ferret out information. Chester kept notebooks full of observations and pulled together a set of tough recommendations that upset lots of folks. Then that superintendent left for a high-prestige district before he took any action. He had left Chester unprotected, and Chester was reassigned to the classroom for a few years.

Now in his early forties, he was wiser after weathering a divorce, high blood pressure, and his father's death. He had remarried and was starting a new life with Trudy's help. Chester was trying to develop a calmer, more balanced approach to work. He and Trudy took real vacations. He was carefully marshaling his resources for a nice retirement. He left work at the office and had a large circle of friends away from work. He worked well with Haskell Dunn, the principal of Westside Middle School.

Still, Chester often talked to Trudy about his frustrations with administration. Trudy listened patiently to his far-ranging litany of disappointments: "School's no fun now, 'cause everyone's labeled as racist. My principal, Mr. Dunn, can be racist—but that's okay because he's Black. I'd be better off if we still had the old boy network. Now we have appointments by race and gender quotas. Oh, there's no formal policy, but when one Black leaves, another is appointed—same with women. Mostly, it's social climbing parents who go to the school board and hire a lawyer to get their way. I have to deal with parents who are ready to call the superintendent over a broken tape player. I'm a conservative Republican; I don't agree with the trend toward mediocrity in schools. The curriculum is diluted as we have to deal with things like AIDS and drugs. Special education policy is well intended but interpreted by the courts to absurdity. Funding cuts ruin morale—then the district deals with the cuts by taking away supplies, by furloughing personnel—but they don't touch the athletic program. I can't keep quiet about absurdities. The State School Board decreed that we'd have criterion-referenced testing but provided no time to set the program up and none of the required equipment and prompts for the tests. One of the illustrations for a fifth-grade test item included a nude."

Chester was not sure he could keep quiet over these issues. Still, he would like to end his career in education as a middle school principal. That would make it all worthwhile; that would have made his father proud. Methodically working with the system and helping quietly as Mr. Dunn prepared to retire should put him in the lead when the next principalship opened up. Going with the flow and cooperating with the ideas of more powerful administrators at the districtwide meetings and keeping things quiet and calm at the middle school for Mr. Dunn's last 2 years should do the trick.

So how could he even consider letting one custodian ruin his plans? His blood pressure escalated as Chester told Trudy janitor stories, mixing anger with humor. He laughed at himself for getting so upset but remained upset. Mr. Dunn and his previous supervisors had always given Chester good yearly evaluations. Often they mentioned his sense of humor and his energy as great assets for dealing with the intense problems he faced. However, Mr. Dunn did not appreciate Chester's inclinations to take action. When a teacher performed poorly, he would tell them, bluntly. Mr. Dunn kept talking to him about being more diplomatic, about calming down, and about just keeping things going smoothly. One section on the annual evaluation concerned "interpersonal relations," and Chester knew well that Dunn felt he had weaknesses in that area. Dunn just wanted 2 quiet years before his retirement.

"I follow the Stoic philosophers who said, 'If an act is worth doing, don't be afraid to be seen doing it,' " Chester told Trudy. "The chief of the custodial staff is unbelievably bad. If something breaks, he just turns it off. Fixing it is too much of an inconvenience, not on his agenda. I've formally surveyed his work and shown Dunn the amazingly bad results. Dunn doesn't want to see it, just wants to leave it alone."

Chester was not sure he could leave it alone. Neither was he convinced he was willing to let this damned janitor foul up his last chances for promotion. Had he not already learned and relearned the lesson about blowing whistles to higher-ups who were not going to do anything?

3.3. Overqualified

Belinda Terry did not need to work. Aunt Bea's generous bequest, her smart investments, her supportive but busy husband, and her empty nest meant she could relax and enjoy life as she wished. She was proud of her newly earned Ph.D. in educational administration. The independence and free thinking that came from taking off from work for 2 years to complete her doctoral course work and to write her dissertation had enervated her. A wealth of teaching and administrative experiences filled her résumé. All of this gave Belinda a bewildering and wonderful sense of wide-open opportunity.

She had, however, always worked hard, and she felt guilty about not applying her expertise and talents in one of the local school districts. She had followed along with her husband's job relocation from Iowa to Southern California. She had checked; the three closest districts had tremendous need for her bilingual expertise but only in low-level administrative positions like elementary assistant principal and low-level central office, paper-pushing jobs. In spite of her pride, she interviewed for an assistant principalship in one of the districts. Clearly, she intimidated the principal, 15 years her junior and still earning his master's degree. She did not get the position.

"Help me make good contacts," Belinda pleaded to her old professors from Iowa and close friends in the superintendents' association. The professors' networks did not extend all the way to the West Coast, however, and the superintendents' contacts were even more regional.

Her closest friend spoke frankly. "Face it, Honey, you look 50, and you're not lean, hungry, and eager—you're not anybody's vision of a protégée. Nobody can afford to take the little 2-year vacation you did, then move."

Belinda knew, too, that she *could not resist* showing off her excitement about new theories for leadership, critical theory, and feminist critique; the latest research on inefficiencies in administration; and the continuing debates about the role of schools in reproducing societal inequities. After her one West Coast job interview she told her husband, "I was being *so* careful to try to look downright submissive. I knew the principal was intimidated. But when he asked about what I'd do on the dropout prevention program, I couldn't just say, 'Shucks, I don't know!' So I let loose with a lecture from research and, midstream, I knew I'd done myself in."

She found little delight in her freedom from obligations or her comfortable investment income. She could not throw herself into volunteer work the way she had buried herself in her previous jobs. Belinda continued to read academic journals and reports on policy issues in education because that seemed to keep her in touch and involved. There must be a way to break in, at an appropriate level, so she could apply her knowledge and energy. She just had to find the right angle.

3.4. The Irresponsible Friend

As a first-year assistant principal in the high school where he had spent his years as a teacher, George found himself in trouble. George and Charles had been friends since they had started teaching in the English department at Garfield High School in 1983. Both had just graduated from the university. Charles had been recruited to head up the yearbook staff that year and loved the work. George's mentor was Gertrude Douglas, now an assistant superintendent for administration and planning in the district. As a matter of fact, Gertrude was the reason that George entered administration. She had convinced him to replace her as department chair when she moved into district administration and then had encouraged him to complete his master's degree in school administration.

But now George faced a problem. The bill on his desk from the publisher of the high school yearbook said that Garfield High School owed $3,000 more than the original signed contract stipulated. As yearbook sponsor at Garfield High School, his friend Charles negotiated the contract with the publisher, figured out the selling price, recruited and supervised the student staff, and handled sales and distribution of the finished product. He was, according to Garfield tradition, "Mr. Yearbook." George suspected that the way Charles had renegotiated the deadlines, the number of pages, and the number of color screens accounted for the $3,000 discrepancy. George showed Charles the bill immediately.

"Are you, as yearbook sponsor, authorized to renegotiate a signed contract like this?" George asked.

Charles seemed surprised at the question. "I asked you about it," he told George. "Don't you remember when we talked in November about the great staff I have this year? These kids had a lot of new ideas for campus shots and wanted to include some original student literary and art work. I think we'll have a good chance to win a publisher's award for this year's design."

Seeing the look on George's face, Charles continued. "Come on, George. You know the contract has been written the same way every year since 1963. The only change is how much we pay. This year, knowing the staff we had, I figured we'd change the format. You agreed. In fact, you said, 'Change isn't cheap.'"

"I agreed in principle," sighed George. "But I had no idea it involved changing the contract. Where is the $3,000 going to come from?" Central office personnel would not only hold him responsible but also view him as a poor manager if he asked them to make up the difference.

"Look," Charles replied, "you've always been tight with Gertrude. Use your special pull. Call her and see what she can work out. You're the assistant principal now."

George walked back to his office remembering the advice another administrator had given him. "You're not a teacher anymore," Manny Rodriguez had said. "None of the old loyalties count." Disgusted and angry, he was tempted to walk into the principal's office and confess that he did not feel he could objectively deal with Charles and this problem.

3.5. Making the Transition From Special Education

"I've been a principal for 5 years at the school for the deaf," Sue explained patiently. "I've worked as a teacher in both the regular and special education programs in the public high schools. I've been a regional director of educational programs for the deaf. That involved 42 counties in the eastern part of this state."

Sue was meeting with yet another school district personnel officer to ask why her application for an administrative position had failed to make the "paper cut." Once again, she was not even interviewed for the open administrative positions in this district, middle school principal and director of exceptional education. She had decided to ask for personal interviews after the first few rejection notices several months ago. Most of the administrators she talked to were evasive and seemed eager to get her out of their offices. Dr. Riley, however, seemed to take more interest in her.

"Sue," Dr. Riley said, "I'm going to be blunt. Your résumé is not at all typical. You haven't been in public schools since 1982. For over 10 years you've been involved somehow with the education of the deaf. You know, whether it's right or wrong, the conception is that most advocates for the deaf don't believe in mainstreaming. If you want to come back into regular education, you're going to have to come in like everybody else."

"What do you mean by that, 'like everyone else'?" Sue asked.

"Take a job with a school district, any job, so that people can get to know you," Dr. Riley replied. "After a year or so, once people have seen the quality of your work, start applying for administrative positions. Your experience, while valuable, won't get you in the door as an administrator in most school districts."

Driving home, Sue reviewed her education, her experience, and her options. She had earned a bachelor's degree in history, a master's and a specialist degree in supervision, and she was about to complete her final year of a doctoral program in educational leadership. She had spent 11 years as a high school teacher, 3 years as a regional coordinator, and 5 years as an administrator. True, she had spent the past 10 years in special education programs for the deaf. Why, she wondered, did people think that her experience was somehow limited? Deaf students often had more than one handicap. Some were gifted. Her experiences had made her an expert in school law, state and federal, not just the laws regarding handicapping conditions. Why could others not see that her experiences in special education would make her a strong and informed advocate for all children, particularly the handicapped?

As the parent of a 13-year-old mentally handicapped daughter, Sue felt a strong need to bring informed advocacy to regular education. Application of the "least restrictive environment" ruling did not always take the long-term needs of children into account. However, if to begin again as a public school teacher was the price for reentry into the regular education mainstream, she was not sure she was willing to pay. As a single parent of a college-bound daughter and a handicapped daughter, and as a doctoral student with substantial educational expenses of her own, she knew supporting herself and her children on the salary of a teacher or an assistant principal would be difficult.

"I can stay in special education at my present level or return to regular education and take a lesser position and a cut in salary," Sue thought. The transition from regular education into special education had not been full of roadblocks and gatekeepers. Had she been labeled, just as special education students are labeled? Would a male special educator be similarly labeled and limited? She had taken positions in deaf education to broaden her experience. Would that experience now block her from seeking a superintendency? Why could school districts not see that the atypical person may be just the person they need?

3.6. Responding to the Tap on the Shoulder

"You really ought to go into administration," the young teacher told Alice. "You explain things so well, and you make me feel like I can teach instead of making me feel like I have to pretend I can do it."

Alice smiled and said, "Everyone, *except* administrators, has always told me that. Frankly, I've been thinking about administration a lot lately. After all, I've been teaching for over 15 years."

After the young teacher left, Alice went back to her desk and her plan book. She looked around the classroom and wondered whether she really wanted something else. She loved English literature. Working with 11th graders kept her young. Would leading a school accomplish more than teaching 150 kids every year? "No," she told herself, "that's the wrong question. The correct question is why other teachers think I'd be a better administrator than most of the ones they have worked with." During her 16 years in the classroom, many teachers had joked, "Let me know if you decide to open a school. I'll come to work with you."

"Maybe that's it," thought Alice. "People know I'd work with them rather than expect them to work for me." She decided to talk with her principal.

Mr. Harding was candid. "We need minority women in administration," he told her. "You'd do well."

"Why," asked Alice, "hasn't anyone ever talked to me about my potential? Gary Jones was a third-year teacher, and not even a particularly good one. From the superintendent on down, people tried to convince him to be an administrator. That was 5 years ago, and he's principal of a middle school now. I'm 41 years old. Changing careers now is scary. I'd have to go back to school."

Mr. Harding laughed. "You always told me that you missed taking classes after you finished your master's degree. I would have loved to have stayed in the classroom for a few more years. I felt pushed because I had a family to support. You'd be a fine principal. How can I help?"

Alice drove home that afternoon thinking about how different her own motivation for moving to administration seemed compared with Gary Jones and Mr. Harding. She did not have a burning desire to get ahead or to make more money. She just wanted to do the best she could for children. She wondered if that was enough. Would she be competitive enough to get a principalship? Would others consider her too old to have new ideas and enough energy? Could she really afford to go back to school and learn a new field? Mr. Harding seemed to think that being a member of a minority was an advantage. She was not sure she agreed.

The next day, Mr. Harding told Alice about an assistant principalship available for the next year at a nearby middle school. "You don't have to have any special certification for that," he told her. "I'd be happy to recommend you. The AP slot is a good way to find out if you like administration. If you're interested, why don't you talk to Dr. Glenn over in personnel."

Alice said she would think about it.

"Don't wait too long," Mr. Harding replied. "People need to know you're interested."

3.7. Detentions for Bathroom Time

Andrea Jacobs taught biology at Williamsburg High School. She had worked at Williamsburg several years, and, generally, she had earned the respect of students and faculty. Ms. Jacobs preferred that students not leave her classroom to use the restrooms. Her policy stipulated that students who left during a class period must make up the missed time after school in a 15-minute detention.

Although Assistant Principal Michael Rogero had great respect for Ms. Jacobs's knowledge of biology, he was not sure about her skill at working with teenagers. Here was yet another problem. Steve Belson, a junior and a loner with a surly attitude, felt that Ms. Jacobs had treated him unfairly. He had missed school for 2 days because he was ill, and then the day he returned to school, he had asked to be excused to use the restroom during Ms. Jacobs's class. She had dismissed him with the warning, "You know the rule, Steve. I'll see you for 15 minutes after school today."

However, Steve had not come to detention that afternoon, and Ms. Jacobs had reported his absence to the office. When Michael received the third report of a skipped detention on Steve from Ms. Jacobs, he called Steve into his office. "It's not fair," Steve had argued. "I told her I was sick. Why should I serve detention because I had to leave the room when I was sick?"

Michael tried to explain that Steve was not going to learn much biology from Ms. Jacobs if he put all his energy into fighting her rules, but the argument did not seem to convince Steve. He left the office as soon as Michael gave him a chance.

Within a few days, Ms. Jacobs notified Michael that Steve Belson had skipped detention a fifth time. School policy at

Williamsburg required students who missed five detentions to serve a 1-day in-school suspension. That meant that Steve Belson now became Michael's problem. "I can see the headline in the local paper," Michael groused to one of the guidance counselors, " 'AP Suspends Student for Going to the Bathroom.' The media will probably carry the story for a week because not much else is happening in town right now."

At the same time, he knew that people in the community believed in strict discipline. One third of the parents were associated with the military base nearby.

He felt trapped. If he failed to enforce the rule, Andrea Jacobs would claim that he was not doing his job and that he was not supporting the teachers. If he did, he was suspending a student for what he felt was a legitimate absence from the classroom. He really did not know what to do or how to act in the best interest of the student, the teacher, and the school. And, frankly, he cared about whether he looked good. Michael knew people were watching him. Just last week, the superintendent had taken him aside and said, in a flattering but pointed tone, "Michael, I've got my eye on you."

3.8. You Can't Ask That

No wonder the district employed only one female administrator. When a search committee member asked, "What does your husband do?" Darrah Grandmeier bristled and then made an evasive and humorous remark, hoping to avoid an awkward situation. Another member looked uncomfortable but did not interfere with the line of questioning.

The damned fool persisted. "What's this 'Women in Leadership' thing you did, here on your résumé—that's not some feminist thing, is it?" Darrah patiently and cordially answered the questions. But when he asked, "Do you plan to have children?" Darrah's face reddened with rage and confusion. This was illegal—it was so close to his asking about her birth control methods, so close to sex discrimination. She knew it and he ought to know it. She could be down his neck with a lawsuit in 2 minutes. She felt like walking out. Instead, she avoided the question by talking about her commitment to public school administration. In her indirect way, she stuck by her rights to refuse to discuss her personal life.

When the interview ended, she felt disheartened and violated. Still, she needed this job. And she knew that in every application for every position, people would wonder whether she would be waylaid by pregnancies and they would have to find ways to make up for her absences. Should she have just answered that idiot's question? Should she have brought birth control up first and put them at ease?

She talked it over later with Al, her husband, and her friend Felicia. Both suggested she sue if the committee did not recommend her for the job. Felicia, a labor union activist, did not mince words. "Go for the turkey's gullet!" she said.

Al was supportive, as always. "I'm behind you 100%; I'll understand if you want to walk away from this and take more time looking elsewhere. And I'll fight alongside if you decide to fight." Unlike Felicia, Al understood a few things about what happens to administrative candidates labeled as troublemakers.

Nevertheless, Darrah knew this was only one small incident. Women faced so many subtle barriers and biases, and they seldom garnered enough support to feel comfortable when they did attain administrative positions. Somebody should do something. Maybe she should do something.

3.9. The Stultifying Reprimand

Howard Longreen, the first-year principal of a medium-sized elementary school in a large city, had moved into administration after 12 years in the classroom because he felt teachers deserved good leadership. He had not experienced much of it himself. Rather than complain constantly about the lack of informed and caring leadership, he had decided to put himself on the line.

His 2 years as an assistant principal had gone fairly well. This year, the superintendent had picked him to head a new project in an inner-city school with a totally new and voluntary staff. He and a committee of parents and central office administrators had selected an outstanding staff dedicated to the premise that "all children can learn." They had spent the year doing the groundwork to implement the model for schools developed by James Comer. Morale was high, the kids were doing great, vandalism was way down, parent participation was on the rise, and the community was beginning to understand and respond to student needs. What could go wrong? But something had.

Dr. David Fredrick, dean of the dental school at State University, was a good friend of his father's. Over the holidays, the dean had given Howard a copy of his book *School-Based Delivery Systems* saying, "Your dad's been telling me what a great job you're doing. I know something about Comer and what he's been working on at Yale. You might be interested in a project I headed up in Louisiana. Maybe the school district and the university could work together on something similar."

Howard had read the book with excitement. Inner-city kids do not usually have access to regular dental or medical care, and the book described how to locate a satellite dental clinic in a neighborhood school. Howard looked at his school building for a possible location and discovered that two of the empty classrooms, the result of declining enrollments, would be perfect. He called Dean Fredrick, who had sent over Dr. Bridges, a dental professor who was interested in heading a community outreach project, and two of the professor's students. Howard, Dr. Bridges, and the dental students had looked at the classrooms, and Dr. Bridges thought the location would work. "Let's do it," he had told Howard. "We'll set up the dental clinic first; maybe we can work out the medical aspect in a year or so. We'll serve your students and maybe some other neighboring children. We'll be in the community serving the children where they live."

Howard had inquired about the cost of the proposed partnership. Dr. Bridges said, "We've got the funding. We'll create the clinic. We'll supply the technicians, equipment, and chairs at no cost to the school system other than normal utilities and the cost of the space."

Howard had responded immediately. "Let's write up a proposal and make sure we've got approval on both sides and then send it in."

Putting the proposal together had taken 2 weeks, with input from Howard's staff as well as university personnel. Howard then called the superintendent with the news that he had a dynamite idea. The superintendent said he was interested and asked Howard to "send the proposal through channels." Howard put it in the mail to the assistant superintendent for curriculum and instruction, George Grassle. After 4 weeks passed without any response, Howard had called Dr. Grassle.

"I've taken a look at it," Dr. Grassle had told Howard. "I'm not sure that this is something the district is ready to commit to. I don't see where you've run this by the director of schools. Don't you think you should have sought some district advice before bringing in the university?"

"Look, Dr. Grassle. This is a great opportunity to provide a needed service to our kids. It never occurred to me that you wouldn't be as excited about this opportunity as my staff and I. I can't believe you'd stand in the way."

"You're out of line, Howard," retorted Dr. Grassle. "The school system requires that you speak to the director of schools before writing a proposal. You need to do that before we can respond. Don't call me again until you've talked to the director of schools."

Howard had agreed to meet with the director of schools and asked Dr. Grassle if he would like to attend the meeting. "I'll get hold of Dr. Bridges and Dean Fredrick, the dean of the dental school who wrote the book on this approach. We can make a formal presentation."

The next day, the director of schools had called to tell Howard he need not involve anyone from the university. Howard should himself meet with some central office staff that afternoon.

Howard had gone to the meeting prepared to discuss, to explain, and to promote the plan. He had been completely unprepared for the cold reception he had received from the superintendent, Dr. Grassle, and the director of schools. After the presentation, Dr. Grassle expressed concern that Howard was confusing school business with welfare business. "We're in the business of education," Howard was told. "This is health care. We don't have, nor can we afford to have, the kind of liability insurance we'd be required to have."

Others echoed the same sentiment in different words. "We can't afford to take instructional time from the school day for dental care," the superintendent said.

"Just because Louisiana can get away with something doesn't mean our school board is going to go along with this. How will it look in the papers when we are using classrooms for a dental clinic while we are proposing to build two new schools?" was the question posed by the director of schools.

Finally, the superintendent thanked everyone for their input and asked that Howard remain for a few minutes after the others had left. The superintendent said, "I picked you to head up this model school project because you're good at putting things in place. I don't want a model health clinic. I don't want a school health clinic at all. I want a model school that does what a school is supposed to do, and that, Howard, is teach children. You went way out on a limb with this one. This isn't how we do business in this school district. I don't want to have to explain that to you again."

His voice had softened as he walked with Howard out to the parking lot. "I don't want to dampen your enthusiasm, Howard. Just confine your genius to schooling, and we'll all be happy with you again."

Now Howard was back in his own office paging through the doomed proposal for the clinic. Even as a principal, he was running into a leadership void.

3.10. Too Many Crises, Too Little Time

Barbara Wegner had always been keenly attuned to changes affecting the New Grange School District. The city, like its sister northeastern cities, suffered economically as corporate offices and shopping centers moved to the suburbs. This, combined with the White flight that followed desegregation efforts, resulted in shifts in the student population—from 70% White to 72% minority, with 66% of the children qualifying for free lunch. Ironically, these changing conditions had resulted in increased administrative opportunities for women and minorities across the country. The highly visible and highly paid big-city superintendencies were increasingly held by women and minorities.

New Grange was no different. The city papers noted and commented on every action of "Dr. Judy" from the moment she first became superintendent. Dr. Judith Norton, the city's first African American and its first woman superintendent, had moved slowly but visibly through levels of staff central office positions. She had developed a wide and solid network throughout the New Grange District administrative staff. Dr. Judy knew people, she knew Barbara Wegner, and she trusted the people who had vouched for Barbara.

The changes in New Grange became personal and concrete for Barbara 2 months after Dr. Judy's appointment. Barbara was amazed, shocked, and delighted when she heard that Dr. Judy wanted her for the principalship of George Washington Carver High School.

Barbara had not been an obvious choice. She had spent a long time, over 12 years, as a high school assistant principal. She had stayed because she worked with good people, and New Grange paid administrators well. During those years, she had learned to work within the system and to tolerate the "good old boy" system that seemed to favor the promotions of White males. She enjoyed life. She never married, but she shared a home and a cabin in the mountains with two women friends. She was slowly working on her doctorate at the local university. She was not hungry for promotion, but when Dr. Norton created a new examination system for administrative positions, Barbara had put out extra effort to do well. She found out first through the grapevine, then by official letter, that she was in line for the next principalship that opened up.

"But why Carver?" she had asked one of her friends. "It's 80% Black, and I'm as White as you can get. What a challenge!

It's the biggest high school in the district. There are all those magnet school programs to deal with."

Barbara coped with her initial excitement by starting a diet, scheduling regular manicures, and resolving anew to finish the damned doctorate. She worked through the summer on scheduling and held small group meetings with staff in preparation for the opening of the school year in early September.

By the end of September, she was exhausted, scared, and feeling very vulnerable. Even with all her experience, she had no idea that she would be so lonely and find the work so difficult. First, teachers' legitimate and unresolved complaints about salary and unfulfilled promises came to a head in a strike. She had opened school with television cameras recording the reactions of angry parents who had accompanied the few students who had actually showed up. Few teachers had crossed the picket lines. She covered some classrooms herself, as the two assistant principals and the guidance counselor tried to help out. She agonized over what to say to reporters. She worried about whether she would be able to build a solid professional relationship with the striking teachers to whom she had to represent the central office party line. She worried about students getting out of control with so few adults to provide supervision. Somehow, they muddled through. The strike ended after 6 days, and classes started.

She had just begun to think about how she could repair the damages caused by the strike. However, she never had time to think through or finish anything. Her first meeting today had been with Fritz Webb, the physical education teacher. He had come to her in despair about managing his career and dealing with the increasing evidence that students knew he was gay. Graffiti in the locker rooms and loud whispers among the students were bringing it all to a confrontation, he said.

They had not even begun to talk about what they might do when one of the assistant principals had burst in saying, "Come right now. We've got a fight in the cafeteria!"

As they rushed through the halls, the assistant principal explained that the fight had all the markings of racial conflict. At least 20 boys were involved, Whites against Blacks.

Again, they muddled through. Somehow she and the assistant principal had stopped the fight. They had suspended every student in the vicinity. When Barbara returned to her office, Fritz was gone.

Exhausted, she locked the door, sat down, and burst into tears. She was a failure. She knew she needed help. She also knew that if anyone saw just how badly she needed help, she would be in even more trouble. How could she tell anyone how little she knew about handling these kinds of issues and crises? When her appointment as principal had been announced, people had said, "Great, you'll be terrific" and "We have confidence in you." Well, they should see her now, defeated after less than a month of school. She just wanted to get in her car and drive away. The mountains would be beautiful and very peaceful this time of year.

3.11. Rules Are Meant to Be Followed

During her meetings with the new teachers early in the fall, Principal Janelle Wood had carefully reviewed the student and faculty handbooks for Thomas Jefferson Senior High School, including the rules about testing. Now, as Mary Ann Kincaid, the new assistant principal at Jefferson, reviewed the circumstances surrounding Donald Coombs's confrontation with two freshman girls, Janelle considered whether she had put too much emphasis on the rules and too little emphasis on education.

"I just don't understand Donald," Mary Ann said. "I know he lacks experience, but I would never have done this, even as a first-year teacher."

"He thinks he was just following the rules?" Janelle asked.

"Well, yes, and in a way he was. The rule says that faculty are to monitor examinations, and Donald certainly took the rule seriously. He walked up and down the aisles of his classroom as the first-hour freshmen took the examination. The policy says that faculty should establish clear rules for classroom testing. Donald did that. He handed out a list of rules, and he reminded the students several times that they were not to talk during the exam. If they did, he warned, he would confiscate exam papers and assign those who talked an 'F' on the test. He was clear enough."

"So the students understood they were not to talk," Janelle replied.

"Right, but I'm sure that Angie and Megan weren't thinking about the rules. Both of them had finished their exams. Angie asked Megan if she wanted some gummy bears, and Donald confiscated their exams."

"How would you have handled it in your classroom, Mary Anne? You were a teacher for, what, 11 years? You've dealt with this kind of problem before."

"Well, yes and no. I never had a rule like Donald's for my class, and even if I had felt such a rule were necessary, I'm not sure I would have applied it in this instance. The girls weren't cheating. I feel as if Donald is being too legalistic here, but he doesn't seem to see it that way. He even told me that he intends to base grades in his class partly on whether students follow the rules. And he told me that he's willing to say that to the parents, who are obviously going to want some kind of explanation. Angie and Megan are pretty upset about this. They both have reputations as good students."

"So the question isn't how you would have handled this as a teacher but how, as an assistant principal, you're going to work with Donald, the first-year teacher. What are you going to say to the parents? How are you going to help Donald get himself out of this difficulty?"

"Good questions, Janelle. Are you going to help me out with some answers?"

"I think you can handle it. Just remember that Donald is a novice and that this is a novice's mistake, even if it's one you would have avoided. Try to focus on what you can do to help him understand that you support him but that you're interested in helping him learn to be firm without being rigid."

"Right now he's telling me that we've got to send the right message to kids," Mary Anne replied. "In Donald's view, the right message is that when you break a rule you get punished."

"Let me know what you come up with," was Janelle's only response. "I'm sure you'll figure out how to help him see that his classroom is about more than rules and punishments."

3.12. Firing an Elderly Teacher

Miss Erlandson had taught third grade at Oak View Elementary School for 25 years. The new principal, Jane Wallcott, had heard references to Miss Erlandson from all the veteran staff members. Indeed, she seemed an important part of Oak View. She served as "grandmother" to the younger staff members and "mother" to the ones in their thirties and forties. Miss Erlandson brought cakes and cookies to the faculty lounge every Monday and graciously put the recipes in the mailbox of each staff member who requested them. She listened to the younger teachers talk about child-rearing problems, and she empathized with the older teachers who faced caring for elderly parents. She had even cared for one teacher's school-aged children for 2 weeks when a relative in another state died suddenly. Miss Erlandson presented only one problem. Two weeks after school opened, Jane suspected that Miss Erlandson's third graders were going to have a bad year, and 4 weeks into the school year, Jane knew she was going to have to do something about the situation.

Jane had missed the first clue that something was wrong. On the day she received her class lists, Miss Erlandson had hurried down to the office to talk to Jane. "I never get any students who can read on grade level," she said. Jane assured Miss Erlandson that each of the five third-grade classrooms had an equal number of low-, average-, and high-performing students.

The second indication had come on the first day of school when Jane had visited each of the classrooms to introduce herself, to welcome students back to Oak View, and to wish each class a good school year. Approaching Miss Erlandson's classroom at the end of the primary hall, she had heard the teacher's voice through the closed door. "Sit down and shut up. We won't start until everyone is quiet. If you can't get quiet, I'll send you back to second grade." The children laughed and applauded. When Jane opened the door and stepped into the classroom, she startled the children into silence. Miss Erlandson looked harried, but she seemed to regain her composure while Jane talked to the children. Although Jane was tempted to end with a warning to the class, she resisted out of respect for this veteran teacher.

Jane thought, "It isn't as if I ignored that chaotic beginning." She had made it her practice to drop in on Miss Erlandson's class several times during the first 2 weeks of school. Each time, she became more concerned about what was happening in the classroom as well as what was not happening. The children did not listen to Miss Erlandson at all. Jane could not recall a single time that she had visited the class when the teacher had spoken in the same tone of voice she used with colleagues. She addressed her students in a critical, antagonistic tone.

At the end of the second week, Jane scheduled a conference with Miss Erlandson to discuss her concerns. The conference had not gone as Jane had planned because when Jane asked Miss Erlandson how she thought the beginning of school was going, Miss Erlandson had replied, "Very well. The children are responding as usual. They are so undisciplined these days, which isn't hard to understand when we consider where they come from. But we do have to insist upon our standards, and once they understand I mean business, they will settle down."

The confident smile of this experienced teacher had so disarmed Jane that she replied, "I hope so, and keep up the good work." She had not meant to compliment Miss Erlandson and was not sure how or why those words had come out of her mouth. What she had meant to say was, "I know this is difficult for you, and I can tell you're trying."

The next week, Jane made a point of standing in the primary hall as the students entered the building in the morning. She noticed that most teachers were in their classrooms, and the children went directly into the rooms, hung up their coats and book bags, and got ready for the day. Miss Erlandson waited in the teachers' lounge until about 1 minute before the bell. Then she came out, a cup of coffee in her hand, unlocked the classroom, and waited until the children were quiet and in a single line before she let them in the room. This process took as long as 10 minutes. Throughout, Miss Erlandson snapped at the children. "Behave!" "Be quiet!" "Be still!" "Get in line and shut your mouth!"

Two mornings that week, Jane had completed two 5-minute observations in other primary classrooms before Miss Erlandson got her class out of the hall. On Friday, Miss Erlandson stopped by Jane's office and confided, "This class is a lot rougher than those I've had in the past. It's taking me longer than usual."

During the fourth week, Jane had made a point of visiting the class during instructional times. She observed during reading, math, science, language, and story time. After one of these visits, Miss Erlandson had asked, "Is everything all right? None of the other principals spent so much time in my room."

Jane said, "I'd like to talk with you about my impressions." They scheduled a conference.

This time, Jane was determined to express her concerns. She began the conference by reviewing responses she had heard Miss Erlandson make to student answers. Most had been negative. "That's a dumb answer, Cory. You weren't listening so you didn't even hear the correct question." "Listen to that question again, Shelagh. Try to get it through your thick skull this time." "You might hear what I'm saying to you if you'd wash your ears once in a while."

Jane suggested strongly that these negative comments were related to student behavior. "The children don't feel as if you like them," Jane explained, "so they don't try to please you."

"I've been teaching in this school for many years," Miss Erlandson replied. "I know these children. They don't respect anyone unless they are treated as they are used to being treated at home."

Jane felt as if she and Miss Erlandson had reached an impasse. "Why don't we arrange for you to observe in some other classrooms and see how some other approaches work and encourage different student attitudes and behaviors?" she suggested.

"There's nothing I can learn from the others. I've taught all of them. They don't do anything different from me, anyway.

You're new here; you'll learn what works with these children," Miss Erlandson replied.

"Miss Erlandson," Jane responded. "Are you aware that Kendra's mother believes that her bedwetting is related to the stress that Kendra is feeling in your class? Mrs. Brown said she sent you a note about that a week ago."

"Oh, that. Kendra had an easy second grade where she didn't have to sit still and do seatwork. This is normal until she gets used to my ways. I've explained that to Mrs. Brown."

"Miss Erlandson, I am going to have to insist that we come to an understanding. In my view, your treatment of the children in your classroom is inconsistent with good teaching. I can't believe you don't know that."

Miss Erlandson dabbed at the sudden tears in her eyes. "I'm doing my best," she said. "If you think I should observe, I'll observe. But I don't know what I'm going to learn from the other teachers. I taught them everything I know about teaching."

Miss Erlandson was apparently right about that. Two weeks later, after Miss Erlandson had observed several primary classes, Jane could neither see nor hear any difference in Miss Erlandson's third graders. Should she continue trying to help Miss Erlandson develop a more caring and considerate tone with the children? Should she begin the long and tedious process of firing this elderly woman who mothered everyone except the children? Had she overlooked something?

3.13. Meet O'Day's New Principal, "Ms. Goody-Goody"

Rose had started her administrative career late, had waited till her boys left for college. But now she had her chance, at age 45, as the newly appointed principal of O'Day Elementary. Her 20 years as a teacher in several grades in two different states gave her broad experience. She had tested her administrative sense in long conversations with Hilda Spence, her best friend, neighbor, and a longtime school board member with a good feel for the values and concerns in the community. She felt well prepared.

O'Day Elementary was a challenge, however. Most of the children came from stable, blue-collar families that held tight to old assumptions. Most believed that "a woman's place is in the home," even though many of the wives held full-time jobs. Most subscribed to "spare the rod and spoil the child" thinking. Rose had a sense of the distance between community values and her own when she took the job, but one day her friend Hilda spelled out the harsh realities.

"Let me give it to you straight, Rose. Now, I never said this to you, but you've got to spank at least one kid; that's all there is to it. You got to show some grit. Your nickname is Ms. Goody-Goody. Teachers are saying you're not tough enough. They were comfortable with Mr. Preston's way. Many of them were against you from the beginning."

"But that's harsh," Rose protested. "My doctoral courses emphasize child development. We have statewide initiatives on alternative discipline. We talk about supporting women in leadership. You're saying that I should throw all that aside and spank a child? God, Hilda, how cynical can you be? Shouldn't I offer a better model for this community? And isn't this just outright sexism? Are you saying that just because I'm 5 feet tall and have soprano voice, I won't be regarded as a leader unless I act tough like a man?"

"Calm down," Hilda replied. "I'm just trying to help; I want you to succeed. Remember, I'm the one who spoke up at the board meeting and convinced the chairman that you could handle O'Day. Come to think of it, he was saying then that you might be too soft, too middle-class—he's the one who said maybe you'd taken too many university courses. So this is nothing new. Trust me, you should never ignore the whispered nicknames assigned to you. And O'Day parents don't want to hear your speeches about the affective and emotional development of their children. They won't be on your side until you show them that you'll make their kids respect authority and use the methods they understand."

Rose argued with Hilda a while longer, but halfheartedly. Hilda had never steered her wrong, and she certainly knew the community that kept reelecting her. Nonetheless, Rose felt that most of the children she saw for discipline really just needed cooling-off time. Often their actions were just natural self-expression. Besides, she was not in education to hurt kids, not even one. Could she convince teachers and parents her approach would work if given the chance and still survive her first year as principal at O'Day? Would the nicknames get worse?

Reflecting on Issues of Entry: Questions and Considerations

In the section that follows, ideas are presented that may be used to discuss each case. Several questions are raised about each of the cases. A more extended consideration or two is included at the end of each set of case materials.

Case 3.1. Could She Turn It Down?

1. What considerations argue for and against Yvonne's taking the position as assistant principal? Which considerations seem the most important to Yvonne? How do her career objectives influence her decision?
2. How would Yvonne know whether she had been selected for the assistant principalship primarily because she is a woman? Does it matter? Under what conditions should women worry about being selected as a token?
3. How can a job aspirant determine whether a situation is impossible? What factors or considerations would make success impossible in a particular position?
4. Is Yvonne right to be concerned about working for someone she has not met?
5. Consider the representation of women in secondary administration. Has the proportion of women in these positions increased or decreased over the past 20 years? Are women more strongly represented in some kinds and levels of positions at the secondary level than others?
6. Consider the issues that Yvonne may have discussed with her husband. What kinds of support and understanding do administrators need from spouses and significant others? Role-play an example of such a conversation.

Case 3.2. Whistle-Blowing

1. What do Chester's frustrations reveal about his personal values and commitments?
2. Given what you know about Chester from this case, do you believe he would be an effective middle school principal? Support your opinion. What additional information about him would be helpful?
3. What advice would you give Chester regarding the chief of the custodial staff? Although we know little about what the custodian has done, try to relate your answer to this question to the nature of the custodian's failures.
4. Consider the difficulties of being a whistle-blower in any organization. What possible consequences does any whistle-blower risk? What are the possible payoffs? You may wish to investigate the lives of famous whistle-blowers such as "Deep Throat" in the Watergate incident, Frank Serpico with the New York City Police Department, or Karen Silkwood. Are whistle-blowers in education likely to be treated differently than those in other fields?

Case 3.3. Overqualified

1. What are the hazards in taking a job for which one is overqualified? Under what circumstances is this advisable?
2. Should aspiring administrators conceal what they know in order to obtain a position? Is this ethical behavior?
3. What advice would you give Belinda about entry into administration in a new state? What contacts should she make? Develop a specific plan of action for her.
4. Consider the difficulties of two-career families. What, if any, are the obligations of businesses and schools for providing employment to both partners in two-career relationships? What arrangements have couples made when one is forced to move?
5. Consider the factors in school administration that encourage and discourage geographic mobility. How does school administration compare with other professions in this regard?

Case 3.4. The Irresponsible Friend

1. Should Charles have suggested that George talk to Gertrude? Was this suggestion out of line?
2. Should George ask Gertrude for help? Develop an argument to support your answer.
3. Is George correct in assuming that the $3,000 overrun will influence others' perceptions of his administrative abilities? Discuss your answer.
4. To what degree is Charles responsible for the overrun? Has he set his friend up here?
5. What could George have done to avoid getting into the problem he now faces? What were his responsibilities for monitoring the cost of the yearbook?
6. Consider the adjustments that novice administrators must make as they leave teaching and move into administrative positions. What conflicts in loyalty are they likely to feel? Can administrators and teachers be friends?

Case 3.5. Making the Transition From Special Education

1. Is it advisable for candidates to seek the reasons why they were not interviewed or recommended for a position? Suggest several ways this might be done.
2. Sue seeks to make a lateral move, from an administrative position in special education to one in regular education, and, at the same time, to obtain an administrative position in a school district in which she is not currently employed. Which of these moves do you think is more difficult? Why?
3. Is Dr. Riley's advice sound? Why or why not? What other options does Sue have?
4. Is Sue right that administrators are tracked in ways similar to those in which students are tracked? What evidence of mobility or lack of mobility among regular education, special education, vocational education, community education, and other programmatic areas can you find?
5. Consider the opportunities for lateral moves in school administration, such as a move from a staff to a line position with the same approximate salary, a move from elementary-

Entry Into School Leadership 61

to secondary-level administration, or a move from one programmatic area to another as described in Question 4. Interview people who have made such moves and describe the barriers to moves such as these and the opportunities such moves provide.
6. Consider the kinds of career moves that all employees, including educators, may be required to make in the course of a professional career. What kinds of career moves might administrators consider, including moves outside of education? How would a school administrator investigate career possibilities in other fields?

Case 3.6. Responding to the Tap on the Shoulder

1. What opportunities in administration are available to experienced teachers such as Alice? What career objectives seem most realistic and appropriate?
2. Alice seemed to assume that it takes a tap on the shoulder from an administrator to validate her capacity to be in administration. Is she right? Does one have to be chosen?
3. Should Mr. Harding have recognized Alice's interest and capabilities in administration and talked to her first?
4. Consider what obligations Mr. Harding, as principal, has to the teachers in the school regarding their professional development and career plans. Talk to some experienced administrators about how they provide assistance to those who they feel would be effective administrators.
5. Consider the fact that advancement in teaching often requires leaving the classroom. What leadership opportunities might administrators provide for teachers who remain in classroom settings?

Case 3.7. Detentions for Bathroom Time

1. Andrea Jacobs has classroom rules that Michael Rogero does not agree with. Are Mrs. Jacobs's rules fair?
2. Should Michael have discussed Andrea Jacobs's rules with her prior to the incident described in this case? If so, develop a script for this conversation or role-play the exchange.

3. Is Michael responsible for enforcing Andrea's rules, even when he considers them unfair? How might he have intervened earlier to avoid this conflict? Should he have done so?
4. Consider Michael's dual concerns, that teachers perceive him as doing his job well and that his superiors view him as effective. Which of these concerns is most important if Michael wishes to retain his present job? Which is most important if Michael wishes to be promoted? If the answers to these two questions are different, what does that imply about success in school administration?

Case 3.8. You Can't Ask That

1. Is Darrah right that there are many subtle barriers and biases against women? What barriers and biases are referenced in this case? What others warrant consideration? Which have been supported by your personal experience? Which are supported by literature in the field?
2. What are the legal parameters for the questions that can be asked in a job interview? Did the search committee member violate the law in the questions he asked? If so, in what ways?
3. The committee member suggests that Darrah may be a feminist and that, if she is, he would be concerned. What different approaches might Darrah have taken in responding to his question? What approach would you recommend?
4. Should women of childbearing age introduce their intentions regarding children into job interviews? If so, role-play how this might be done.
5. Are these issues more likely to be raised in education than in other fields of employment? Why or why not?
6. Would you recommend that Darrah sue if she does not get the job? Support your answer.
7. Consider the guidelines that schools and school districts should provide to those conducting job interviews. Develop a list of guidelines, or examine and critique a list of guidelines already in use in a school or a school district.

Entry Into School Leadership 63

Case 3.9. The Stultifying Reprimand

1. Is Howard correct in concluding that the administrators to whom he reports demonstrated poor leadership in this incident? What evidence supports your position? How might the superintendent justify his actions?
2. What assumptions about the functions of schools are implied in Howard's actions and statements and in those of the superintendent of schools? Do you agree with either of these sets of assumptions, or do you have a different personal set of assumptions about the functions of schools? Make your own assumptions explicit.
3. Did Howard err in the procedures he used for developing the proposal for the dental clinic? If so, where did he err? What appropriate procedures did he use?
4. Consider the relationships among schools and universities and among schools and other community agencies. What models are available for integrating social services for children and families? Are any of these approaches being used in schools in your region? If so, with what results?

Case 3.10. Too Many Crises, Too Little Time

1. What difficult issues has Barbara confronted in her first few months as a principal?
2. Is Barbara a failure? What advice would you give her?
3. To what degree would her long experience as an assistant principal prepare her for handling these issues?
4. Is it a mistake to appoint a White woman as principal of a large minority high school? What strengths did Barbara bring to the position? What difficulties were built into this appointment?
5. Consider the responsibilities of principals for dealing with strikes and striking teachers. How could novice principals be prepared for handling these responsibilities?
6. Consider the responsibilities of principals for working with the media. How could novice principals be prepared for

handling these responsibilities? Interview experienced principals about the procedures they use in dealing with the media.

Case 3.11. Rules Are Meant to Be Followed

1. What assumptions about rules are implied in Donald Coombs's actions and statements and in those of Mary Ann Kincaid? Do you agree with either of these sets of assumptions, or do you have a different personal set of assumptions about rules? Make your own assumptions about rules explicit.
2. What advice would you give Mary Ann for dealing with Donald on this issue?
3. Janelle may ultimately have to handle this problem. Should she have been more helpful to Mary Ann? If so, in what ways could she have been helpful? If not, why not?
4. Consider the typical problems of beginning teachers and the responsibilities of department and grade-level chairs and building administrators for providing support and guidance to beginning teachers. You may wish to interview one or more building-level administrators about the ways they provide support to novice teachers.

Case 3.12. Firing an Elderly Teacher

1. What should Jane do? What advice would you give her for working (or not working) with Miss Erlandson?
2. Did Jane proceed appropriately in trying to understand Miss Erlandson's teaching methods and approaches to children? Explain your answer.
3. Should an experienced teacher such as Miss Erlandson be treated differently than a novice, but similarly ineffective, teacher? What, if any, special responsibilities do school administrators have to those who have worked in the school district for a long period of time?
4. What assumptions about children and how children learn are implied in Miss Erlandson's actions and statements and in those of Jane Wallcott? Do you agree with either of these sets of assumptions, or do you have a different personal set

Entry Into School Leadership 65

of assumptions about children and learning? Make your own assumptions explicit.
5. Consider the procedures that principals must use to remove a teacher from the classroom. Investigate the state and federal laws, school district policies, and collective bargaining agreements that govern termination of teachers in a school district in your region.

Case 3.13. Meet O'Day's New Principal, "Ms. Goody-Goody"

1. How important is it that an administrator agree with the discipline policy in effect in a particular school or school district? How might discipline policies vary from one school or school district to another? What can administrators do if they disagree with particular aspects of a discipline policy?
2. Is this one of those impossible situations referred to in Case 3.1, a mismatch between Rose and the school community? If so, is there anything that Rose can do about it? How might she communicate with the parents at O'Day?
3. Consider the relationships between the economic levels and educational backgrounds of parents and the culture and climate of schools. Do schools that serve middle-class clientele differ from schools that serve lower and higher income groups? If so, how? What support can you find for your assertions? Look, for example, at studies by Popkewitz, Tabachnick, and Wehlage (1982) and Rutter, Maughan, Mortimore, Outson, and Smith (1979).
4. Consider whether different kinds of schools require different kinds of administrators. What factors about each are important? Investigate the uses and limitations of targeted selection.

4

Equity Issues in School Leadership

School administrators often face conflicts in values and dilemmas that resist resolution. Issues of equity, however, are often particularly difficult for school administrators. Equity does not mean treating everyone equally. Equity, rather, means providing for each child educational opportunity that is appropriate, given the needs of that child. Most children do not need medical attention at school, but some children do. Equal treatment in this instance, that is, providing medical attention to all or to none, would violate our notions of fairness.

Equity is often about redressing societal ills such as race and gender bias. The issues are sometimes subtle. People often disagree on claims of legitimate needs, and administrators must frequently negotiate between the needs of the organization and the needs of individuals. In the cases that follow, issues of equity are explored, including equity in access to administrative positions and equity in the provision of services to children.

Case Studies of Equity Issues

4.1. Equity, Access, and Assessment

Darryl Hill had been associate principal at Ferndale High School for 8 years when Elaine Ellender, his friend and boss, walked into his office one fall day to tell him of her plan to retire from the principalship at the end of the school year. "I've bought some land on a river in the mountains, and I plan to take up trout fishing again," she said. "Jed and I did a lot of it before his heart attack. I love the students and the faculty here, but I think it is time for me to retire and let younger folks take over. Of course, I will recommend you for principal. I'll be available whenever you need me."

Elaine hurried back to her office to avoid the students who would flood the hall when the bell rang. She thought about Darryl, an African American in his early forties, a lifelong resident of the area who knew many of the students and their families in the African-American community. Well liked and respected by nearly everyone, he had been particularly successful as a role model for young Black men. Three from the previous year's graduating class were education majors as a result of his influence, and Eddie Lawrence, the new science teacher, was an alumnus who returned "to learn from Mr. Hill."

"So," Elaine said to herself as she pulled a dead leaf from the philodendron that hung near her chair, "only one more hurdle: the new superintendent and his concern with 'objective' measures of administrative potential. He'll probably insist that we send Darryl to the Leadership Assessment Center. As far as I'm concerned, that's a waste of district money and Darryl's time."

The following Thursday Elaine met with Superintendent Howard at the district office. After telling him of her decision to retire, she recommended he name Darryl Hill as her replacement as soon as possible. "That will make the transition as smooth as possible," she said. "I'm sure the school community will be very supportive of Darryl's appointment."

"How strong an evaluation did Mr. Hill receive from the Leadership Assessment Center?" the superintendent asked.

"He's never been through the program," Elaine answered. She recalled that she had suggested it to him once, but Darryl had declined. He had read a great deal of research on testing for his master's thesis, and he objected to what he called "false attempts at objectivity that financially support test designers."

"You heard me say before, Elaine, that I don't believe in promoting from within the district unless the candidate also performs well in objective tests of potential. Otherwise, school districts can become too inbred and promote people for reasons other than administrative ability."

"I understand your position, Michael, but Darryl Hill is a natural for this position," Elaine replied. "It's important that we have more minorities represented in administration in this district. Darryl's a local person. He lives in the community. He serves as a role model and a reality check. Because he knows the kids and their families, they can't easily con him. He senses when they're shooting him a line. The assessment center can't measure those qualities that are much more important for success in this job than skill in written and oral communication and the technicalities of management."

"I'm not making any exceptions," the superintendent responded. "If Hill is as strong as you claim, the assessment will only confirm that."

As Elaine walked to her car, she wondered what Darryl's reaction would be. She knew that he could handle every aspect of the principalship and that his personality, kindness, and concern for children were strengths impossible to measure with simulations and survey instruments. She also suspected that he would be reluctant to participate in a process in which he had so little confidence.

Elaine was right. When she told Darryl that the superintendent insisted that all administrative candidates complete the Leadership Assessment, he repeated all the reasons why standardized testing fails to measure what is important about learning and why minorities had been particularly ill served by efforts to quantify and objectify performance measures. "How can I submit myself to a process I don't believe in?" he asked.

She tried to reassure him. "I know how you feel, but to retain this privilege of serving young people, you'll have to jump through certain hoops. Don't lose your focus on that. You should do whatever is necessary. What is best for the children should remain foremost in your thoughts, and you, Darryl, are best for these children. With your permission, I'll make the arrangements."

"You always know how to win an argument, Elaine. Sometimes I wish you didn't know my most vulnerable spot."

"No one could possibly miss that someone like you is in this field because he loves kids," she replied.

Several weeks later Elaine received a telephone call from Superintendent Howard. "I have decided to advertise the principalship at Ferndale High School rather than appoint from within the district," he said. "Mr. Hill's scores from the Leadership Assessment Center were not what we would like to see in this district. His communication skills scores and leadership profile were not within the center's parameters for successful administrative candidates."

"But he communicates wonderfully with the students and the parents in this community. Doesn't that count?" Elaine asked.

"Elaine, I've made my decision. We'll advertise the position. I expect you to work with our personnel department in developing the recruitment materials."

Elaine hung by the telephone. She would have to tell Darryl, and she already knew how disappointed and angry he would be. She would have a hard time supporting the superintendent's decision because she really did not understand it herself. Darryl would make a perfect principal for Ferndale High School.

4.2. Peabody's Blue-Ribbon Task Force

Marge Powers, principal of Peabody High School, had been alarmed at the end of fall semester when she reviewed term grades. A smaller percentage of students qualified for the honor roll. A higher proportion of students received one or more Ds and Fs. Average grades had declined, particularly in the freshman and sophomore classes. She knew that parents would be concerned, particularly because the change in school boundaries that took effect in the fall had nearly doubled the size of the student body and had tripled the percentage of minority children the school served.

Marge decided that she should inform parents about the situation and assure them that the lower grades were most likely temporary, a result of the numerous adjustments that students and teachers had to make to the new Peabody High. She drafted a letter describing the trends she had noted and included a summary of the descriptive statistics she had reviewed. She asked parents to help their children by monitoring homework, working to improve study habits, and talking about changes at the school. She was pleased with the letter and confident that involving parents in the problem and possible solutions would help build a sense of community around the school.

She was not prepared, however, for the reaction of Darwin Hawkes, editor of the local newspaper and parent of Jeffery, an 11th grader. Mr. Hawkes had reviewed the statistical data Marge had included with her letter and noted a distinct pattern of low performance by minority students. In his subsequent editorial, he questioned whether parents could and should support a school system that was so obviously failing a segment of the population. He concluded his editorial with these words: "The issue is not whether children are failing. The issue is whether the schools are failing our children."

Mr. Hawkes's words became the theme of the next school board meeting as several African-American parents and community leaders carried their concerns to the board. Reverend Ed House, minister of the Abbysynia Missionary Baptist Church, seemed to speak for many in the audience when he called for a study of the quality of education being offered to all children in the school district, but particularly to minority children at Peabody High School. "Our children deserve better than they are getting," he told the board members. "And we intend to see that they get the high-quality education they deserve." Listening in the audience, Dr. Powers knew she had to respond to the minority community's concerns.

She responded with a second letter, this one announcing the formation of the Peabody Blue-Ribbon Task Force on Quality Education to address the interests of all children. The task force, she noted, should represent the entire community. She concluded her letter with a request for volunteers.

Two days after she mailed the letter, Marge received a telephone call from Mike Rayner. Mr. Rayner was direct. "I haven't had a chance to meet you, but I am an executive at State Bank and Trust, and I have three children in the local schools. I am also a member of Abbysynia Missionary Baptist Church. Reverend House talked to me last night about the school board meeting and about serving as a member of the Peabody Task Force. As an African American, I am quite concerned about quality schooling for both minority and nonminority children. I would like to do something to help. The bank encourages its employees to participate in the community, and this is something I would like to do."

Marge did not hesitate in her reply. "Mr. Rayner, you are a gift from above. I've heard of your work as president of the parents' group at Greene Middle School, and I would be delighted to include you as a member of the task force. Perhaps you'd even be willing to serve as chair, though I'm afraid that might take quite a bit of your time."

"That's quite all right, as long as I have your assurance that our efforts will receive careful consideration from the school board, school district administrators, and Peabody's School Governance Committee."

"You can count on it," Marge replied. "Is there some time this week that we could meet to discuss your thoughts on how we might best proceed with formation of the task force?"

When Marge met with Mike Rayner 2 days later, she was impressed with his sincerity and his commitment. Although not a politician or a policymaker, Mike was determined to unite the African-American community around the issue of quality education for minority children. He described to Marge some of his experiences growing up in a segregated world until he entered high school. "I can remember discussing change in a high school sociology class. One of the students asked the minority kids in the class why we had come to a school where we knew we weren't wanted. One of the Black girls answered, 'Education is important to me. Until I came here, I didn't realize how much I was missing.' Things are still missing for my children, Dr. Powers, and that is why I am eager to give my time as a volunteer to a community that hasn't met their needs."

The task force met nearly every week during the next 4 months, with Mike Rayner providing leadership and a sense of direction. Marge, in a supporting role, provided the task force with additional data and helped them examine patterns and trends. She also encouraged them to meet with teachers and other personnel to discuss possible interpretations of the data. Marge knew she was not the only person occasionally uncomfortable with the task force's focus on racial issues, but Mike always framed the discussion with concern about the success of all children. Task force members slowly reached consensus on the need to address explicitly racial issues in the school district and at Peabody High.

Just as the task force began to draft its recommendations, Superintendent of Schools John Haller asked Marge for an update. Marge told him that members of the task force were drafting a position paper on quality education and that she was fairly sure they would recommend separate reporting of student achievement scores, attendance data, and disciplinary actions for minority and nonminority children at Peabody High School. When the superintendent asked what she felt the separate results would show, Marge said that minority students historically scored substantially below majority students in the district and that a higher percentage of minority students were involved in some sort of disciplinary procedure in any term. Now that Peabody High enrolled nearly as many minority students as majority students, she expected that separate reporting of the data for minority children would initially, at least, provide an unflattering picture of Peabody.

Superintendent Haller did not respond for several minutes but quietly stared out his office window. Then he said, "Can't you stop them? The board has other issues it needs to address. This one will be divisive. We don't need this now."

"But I've promised task force members that everyone will take their work seriously. They have invested months of work in this report. I can't just tell them to forget it."

"Of course you can't," Superintendent Haller replied. "But you'll figure out something. Give it some thought, and let me know what you come up with."

The conversation was clearly over. That was just as well. At the moment, Marge Powers was speechless and confused. What was she going to report to Mike Rayner and the other members of the task force?

4.3. But What About Cultural Diversity?

When Ann Kim Lee first saw the possibilities as Rockville Senior High School's assistant principal, she was excited and determined to use everything she had learned about the spreading movement for multiculturalism during her course work and her administrative internship the year before. "If only I can help bring to this school some of what I experienced in Boston," she thought as she unpacked books in her new office.

Of the several classes Ann had observed as part of her administrative training, her favorite had been a large section of senior studies taught by four teachers. The teachers reflected the diversity of the student body: George Venable, an African-American history teacher; Yvonne Hernandez, a Hispanic science teacher; Marie Vu, an Asian-American mathematics teacher; and Merv Franklin, a White English teacher. In a series of class sessions, they had developed materials around the theme "Cherishing the Land." When asked to describe their heritages, students told stories and described rituals related to the land. During one of the sessions, the principal, Delores Garrison, had joined the group. Wearing a flowing skirt of African fabric, beads, and a small cloth hat, she had presented an interpretive reading of poems written by several former students. Pat Lightfoot, the assistant principal, had also participated by telling stories from the Narragansett tribe. Both Delores and Pat were often involved in classes, but they were particularly supportive of this exploration of heritage and diversity. The whole school, in fact, seemed to encourage the celebration of differences.

Her goal now was to bring such multicultural curriculum, pedagogy, and modeling to Rockville. "Rockville sure needs it," Ann thought as she took the last books from the boxes. "Mr. Pritchard seems as if he'll be a good manager, and I'm eager to get started."

John Pritchard had been principal at Rockville for 9 years. He had grown up in the area and had taught algebra and then been assistant principal at the high school before he became the principal. Ann's background in curriculum had impressed him, he said during the interview, as had her energetic pursuit of the position. She had noticed, however, that his face went blank as she talked about her ideas for multicultural projects. At the time, Ann found this strange. She knew from reading a description of the school district that Rockville's students spoke 14 different languages.

Several days after Ann's arrival, Mr. Pritchard met with her to discuss areas of responsibility. He gave her lunchroom and bus duty, and he showed her the standardized form used to evaluate teachers. "I handle the Gifted Program and evaluate those teachers myself," he said. "The others are up to you. Just do the best you can and try to be as supportive as possible. The teachers work hard, but the slower kids don't respond much." He said nothing about curriculum projects, language differences, or innovation. Ann tried again to introduce the topic of using her curriculum ideas by describing some of the classes she had observed in Boston. Mr. Pritchard listened politely but made no response.

That night she telephoned an old friend. "Sally, I don't think I made the right choice. The teachers seem competent enough, but there's none of the excitement I felt in Boston. I was hired, I was told, because I understand curriculum, but my understanding of curriculum isn't of much use in the lunchroom. And the only times I've heard diversity mentioned here, people refer to it as a problem. The principal seems interested only in the Gifted Program and those teachers and students. It's as if he's given up on a whole range of kids, just put them under a 'deficiency' label and moved on. I know there's someone in the district with money and responsibility for work with multilingual kids. Someone must be tuned into the testing issues for children with different ethnic backgrounds."

Her friend advised patience, and Ann had to agree that she had no other choice.

Several weeks later, Ann approached Mr. Pritchard about sponsoring a cultural festival for the school. He was skeptical: "Some of our students have no money for projects and no time outside of school to work on them. Any time we try a school-wide activity like that, it turns into a disaster."

He had not said she could not do it. She could go ahead without his support by identifying a few teachers and some students she could count on and find a way to begin. She could go around Pritchard and talk to folks in central office. But she had to do something. "I can't just sit here and do nothing, not with all this potential and need," she thought.

She had an uneasy feeling, though, that although some people in Rockville might see her as the champion of diversity, others would see an outsider, Yankee pain-in-the-neck.

4.4. "Sticks and Stones May Break My Bones and Names Can Really Hurt Me"

"You're just a damned Oreo." The irate father's words hit hard—another jabbing wound for Michael Brown. Last Christmas he had had the same feeling when his father-in-law, in a general tirade about young people today, had turned to him and said, "People like you go off to fame and fortune and forget what it's like back home with your own people." Now the ringleader of an African-American parents' group was yelling at him, accusing him of "selling out" his race, of placating them to please "whitey" and advance his own interests.

Mike thought about the incident several times over the next few weeks. He looked for an understanding confidante to discuss his confusion. As the only minority principal, he occupied a lonely position. He wished he could talk with Ted Hess, the other middle school principal. He suspected that Ted was experiencing his own personal struggles, but they found talking on a personal level difficult.

Michael usually held himself back from thinking about the racial issues that rumbled around in his subconscious. Years before, during his student teaching experience, he learned that people became very uncomfortable when he dropped the slightest hint that the curriculum should include more on Black culture. As time passed, he learned to avoid raising issues about the favorable bias for White male administrators. Doc Berger, his first mentor, had told him he would be able to do so much more for young Black children by getting himself into good positions and working behind the scenes than by challenging the system and alienating people. He wondered whether Doc Berger had spent all those hours helping him with his dissertation because then the university could count Mike among their minority doctoral graduates and Doc Berger would look good for having helped him through.

In spite of his occasional cynicism, Mike had worked hard to become a principal. He was proud that he could provide his four children with a thoroughly middle-class upbringing, could afford to send them to good colleges. He had, in fact, followed Doc Berger's advice. As he became known in the school district, he had carefully taken on some of the burgeoning and complex issues other administrators avoided: racism, poverty, the performance of minority children, multiculturalism. Other administrators seemed happy to let him handle such issues. He thought of them as crossing those issues off their lists. They rarely participated and provided only token support, budget, and authority.

That parent's taunting epithet was so unfair. "Am I obliged to be the champion of all the Black community's issues just because I'm Black?" he wondered. As an African American, he knew the issues—no minority professors in his doctoral program, only one minority administrator in his school district. He had heard the cynical murmurs from women assistant principals in the district when he, not one of them, received a promotion. He also knew they held regular "networking" meetings where they discussed their resentment. He read in the literature that Black students needed strong role models, but he noticed that young Black male students rarely hovered around him or expressed admiration.

Mike felt he could not win. The innuendo and name-calling hit close to home. True, nobody was making him *do* anything. He just needed some empathy, some guidance, some understanding comments. Cecile, Mike's wife, had watched him struggle with something he could never articulate. He wondered why he could not just relax and enjoy the privileges he had worked so hard to earn. Why did he carry around this nagging feeling that someone, somewhere, expected him to live with the homeless for the sake of his race?

4.5. Strength to Do the Job

"This isn't where I want to be," Steve Douglas thought to himself as he looked around his small office in the administration building of the Rock County School District. "My strength is working with students, parents, and programs, not dealing with the federal bureaucracy."

For 2 weeks Steve had considered and reconsidered applying for reassignment to his old job as principal of Windy Lakes Elementary School. He felt he was ready. His last incidence of pneumonia had occurred nearly 3 months ago. He was working out at the gym again at least twice a week. The annual shifts of administrative appointments in the district would begin soon. Besides, he had been away from his school for nearly 10 months. In honest moments, he knew he missed being a principal more than anything else he had lost.

He had always separated his professional life and his personal life. He deliberately bought a house away from the school neighborhood. He was active in civic groups and his church, but he and David, his companion, confined their socializing to events and groups that were unlikely to include members of the school community. When members of the Gay and Lesbian Alliance tried to enlist him to use his position and communicate the estrangement and isolation that gay and lesbian students feel, he balked. They just did not understand how a conservative school district might react.

A positive side to the illness, if such were possible, was the support he had received when he became ill. Early in May, on his 42nd birthday, he had taken himself to the hospital. The timing was bad—the end of the school year, a month after he had finished his doctoral degree, 2 months before his assistant principal, Darla, was to move to a principalship in another school. He simply could not breathe. The doctors had tried all standard treatments and, as a last resort, experimental drugs. Other than his doctors, only Darla, David, his family, and his friends in the gay community knew he had AIDS.

Students from Windy Lakes had filled his hospital room with hundreds of handmade cards. They and their parents believed he had lung cancer. When parents and teachers visited him, a few questioned why he was on an isolated floor. Evidently, hospital aides or someone else leaked information. Toward the end of July, the local media called Superintendent Conrad and asked whether it was true that the school district was employing an elementary principal with AIDS. Dr. Conrad's response had been simple: "Why don't you ask him?" No one from the media pursued it.

Darla brought him work and kept the school running. As fall approached, he was still in the hospital, still hooked to intravenous tubes. Clearly, Steve had to talk with the school district about his job. He requested an appointment with Dr. Conrad, who came to his hospital room. Dr. Conrad assured Steve that he would respect his confidentiality, that he would support him in any way he could. He would not lose his job. Dr. Conrad suggested the special assignment that placed Steve in this office in the administration building. Since October he had been on special assignment and responsible for federal grants. Although he trusted Dr. Conrad, Steve suspected that from time to time Dr. Conrad had acted in self-protection as much as in concern for Steve's best interests.

Darla had functioned unofficially as principal until Steve received his reassignment and then officially after that. He always felt, however, that she was filling in until he could get back. They even talked about it that way. "We'll just keep it this way until you're better," she would say. When parents had questioned Darla about his illness, she had been as evasive as Dr. Conrad. As far as Steve knew, students and parents thought that he would be back as soon as his lung cancer was under control.

So now he had the illness under control. The request for reassignment papers sat on his desk. If he just rolled them into the typewriter, he could get back to where he belonged. Of course he had to consider other possibilities. A friend of his had requested reassignment to his old job at a local hospital and was told that reconsideration of his case was likely to include a request for a complete physical "to see if you are able to continue working." Even if the district were to reassign him, he might receive a reassignment he did not want. Although the federal grants job was not very interesting, it was certainly better than the book depository, a possible reassignment he had feared when the pneumonia had flared up 3 months ago. He just was not sure whether to leave the situation alone or to fill out the papers and hope for the best. His decision for the moment was to have another cup of coffee.

4.6. Trusting the Institution

Jackson Montgomery had often given advice to others. "Never trust an institution," he had said. "No institution will provide for your needs as well as you should provide for yourself." Now, 10 years later, he was hurt, angry, and embarrassed in front of his colleagues for having trusted an institution to live up to the promises made to him. "You should have known, Old Buddy," he said to himself. "You really should have known."

Bright and ambitious, Jack had joined the Sunshine County School District as a minority male in a school district that still carried the remnants of separate schools for African-American students. A decade ago, he had thought he could do everything. He had left the university with his course work and his comprehensive examination completed. He had always intended to finish his dissertation, of course, but he was restless, eager to be out in the field where he could make a difference to schools and students. He had not thought the dissertation would pose a problem. He was used to working 6 or 7 days a week. The position of director of special projects in Sunshine County looked liked a way into a school district that had too long ignored the needs of minority children. He had taken the position, worked hard, and had been successful. Five years after he arrived in Sunshine County, he became principal of DuPree Senior High School, a large school with a 99% African-American student population. During his tenure, *Ebony* magazine recognized his urban school as one of few that worked. Such successes did not come easily. He worked long days and long weeks, and the time limit for completion of his dissertation slipped by as he lived his convictions—that Black schools could be known for more than athletics and that African-American students could genuinely learn if given and held to a standard.

In the spring, 9 years after he joined the administration in Sunshine County, he had requested a year's leave of absence to return to his northern university and complete his doctoral degree.

The superintendent of schools was supportive. In fact, he assured Jack that he could return to DuPree as principal after his leave of absence. In the fall of Jack's sabbatical year, the board of education approved $5 million in renovation for DuPree's building and grounds. The superintendent employed him as a consultant to assist with the project and work with the architect. During the last 6 months of his sabbatical, Jack had returned to Sunshine County several times. He had considered the renovation "his baby," part of his personal mission to develop predominantly Black schools into centerpieces in the county's educational program.

While Jack was on leave, a former school district administrator, Spenser Hawkins, served as interim principal at DuPree. Well-known in the district, Hawkins had worked in the county for several years until he left for a superintendency in a neighboring state. When the board of education there bought out Hawkins's contract, the superintendent in Sunshine County brought him back on payroll and placed him at DuPree as acting principal. Jack had never doubted that Hawkins's appointment to the position was temporary. After all, the superintendent had asked him to spend part of his leave making those long drives back to Sunshine County to work on the building project.

What Jack could not have anticipated was that the Sunshine superintendent himself would be fired in a showdown with some powerful members of the school board. When Jack returned to Sunshine County the next May, he met with Darrell Manning, the new superintendent. Jack was eager to talk about the plans he would implement once he resumed his position at DuPree. Manning pointed out that the district's policy ensured Jack a position, not the same position. When Jack replied that the former superintendent had never intended his interim replacement to become permanent, Manning was apologetic but unmoved. Hawkins would remain as principal at DuPree. He offered Jack the principalship at a small alternative school for students unsuccessful in the county's high schools. The school had a reputation for being punitive. Jack could help it become a counseling center, Manning said.

Jack wanted to tell Manning and the Sunshine District to go to hell and to take their counseling center with them. His year of doctoral work had given him contacts in other states. He had been recruited for jobs in other districts, and a few universities had approached him about assistant professorships. He had never questioned whether he should return to Sunshine County and to DuPree. That was his commitment. Where the hell was the county's commitment to him? The county was ignoring everything he had worked for during the past 5 years.

His close friend Julianne was another factor. They had stayed in touch during the year he was away. Every trip he had made back to Sunshine County had strengthened and deepened their relationship. If he walked away from the county, he walked away from Julianne, too.

He was tempted to stay just to show Manning what a mistake he was making. He knew he could make the counseling center work. He knew he could develop an excellent educational program at another school as he had done at DuPree. He wanted to send Manning and the school board a message, but he did not know whether he would send the stronger message by leaving because of the way they had treated him—or staying in spite of the way they had treated him.

4.7. The Humor of *The Hambone*

Nothing in Lynelle Brown's doctoral program in education leadership had prepared her to deal with this volatile situation. In February, she had taken over as principal of Magnolia High School, her first high school principalship. Magnolia, a bedroom community located 15 minutes outside the state capital, seemed a wonderful opportunity. The school had an excellent academic reputation, a motivated faculty, and a modern building. However, disturbing incidents had occurred with some of the high school students, many from affluent professional families. On Halloween, 14 Magnolia students had made headlines in the local newspaper for drunkenness and petty vandalism during a scavenger hunt that required participants to obtain a mailbox, a windshield wiper, a hood ornament from a Mercedes or BMW, and a street sign, among other items.

The adverse publicity had led eventually to the former principal's resignation. Within 2 weeks of Lynelle's appointment, the first issue of an underground newspaper appeared. A concerned teacher, a middle-aged Black woman, had brought a copy of *The Hambone* to Lynelle's office. The teacher had criticized *The Hambone* for its cruel and sexist undertone. Using an automotive metaphor, one article had dismissed the entire English department as "an empty junkyard with nothing left to salvage." Another article classified freshman girls as "hot," "ready," "willing," "used," and "don't bother." Lynelle had thanked the teacher and called Bruce, the budding editor, into her office the next day.

Lynelle had told him that Magnolia would not tolerate this type of irresponsible journalism. Bruce, a senior with an A average, had explained that these articles contained modern humor that "some of the faculty just don't understand." He had asked if any students or parents had complained. Lynelle had admitted she had received only one complaint. Still, she had insisted that Bruce understand that even editors of "underground" newspapers had responsibilities. He left her office thanking her for her trust in him. She had marveled at that later because expressing her trust in Bruce had not been the message she had intended to get across to him.

The next morning she had called Superintendent Brock in the district office and explained her concerns. His response had been troubling. "Lynelle," he had told her, "we hired you to be principal of that school. If you can't do it, just tell me and I'll get someone else. Keep the kids in line, the test scores high, and the community quiet for a while. That's your job." Lynelle felt that was inadequate advice, but she assured the superintendent that she had everything under control and hung up the telephone. In fact, in the next few weeks she did not hear anything more about *The Hambone*. She had considered discussing the newspaper at a meeting of department chairs, but she did not really know what to discuss. Without more issues, she did not have a problem.

However, she did have a problem, Lynelle thought wryly. Earlier that day, Bruce had published and sold in the school halls the May issue of *The Hambone*. This time, nine outraged teachers as well as several parents and students contacted her. The current issue included a column listing the sexual partners of the most popular senior girls. Another article described the requirements for those wishing to apply for welfare. This issue was not only blatantly sexist but also racist. Worst of all, Lynelle learned that morning that Bruce had been selected as the class valedictorian and thus would give the commencement address in 2 weeks.

Lynelle summoned Bruce to her office early the next morning and demanded he cease sales and distribution of *The Hambone* immediately. He had tried to argue, but when she mentioned the inappropriateness of his being named valedictorian after insulting more than 50% of the student body and the faculty with his sexist and racist rag, he had agreed. At 4:00 p.m., his parents were in her office threatening legal action against her and the school district if Bruce were removed as valedictorian. "He earned this by 4 years of hard work and brilliance," his mother had argued. "The newspaper was a kid's prank. What real harm has been done?"

Lynelle had then called the school district's attorney, who advised her that she did not have a case. "Lay low and see what happens when the dust settles," he said.

Two stories appeared in the local newspaper about *The Hambone* and its bigoted articles in the days between release of the May issue and graduation. Students seemed even more upset than the community. Lynelle learned that all 20 of the Black seniors in the class had threatened to walk out if Bruce spoke. Lynelle was appalled. "Can I save graduation?" she wondered. "What is my responsibility? Who is my responsibility? What could I have done to have prevented this from ever happening?"

4.8. Potty Duty

One of Maria Chavez's first projects as the new principal of Bay Elementary School was to read through the cumulative files of children in the Special Education Program. She wanted to know the ages of students and their disabilities to understand the accommodations the school must make. During the reading, the records of an academically gifted rising third grader with degenerative osteoporosis caught her interest. Jennifer Godwin, at Bay since kindergarten, had only recently been diagnosed as having this condition. She had suffered a broken leg and two broken arms during kindergarten and first grade. Her doctor, suspecting something other than clumsiness, had conducted several tests. The prognosis had indicated that broken bones were going to be part of this child's life. Maria read, with growing concern, that Jennifer had broken her arm again and had broken a wrist during the second grade. Both accidents had occurred when the child attempted to get on or off the toilet. This had led to a meeting of the Child Study Committee within the school on Jennifer's behalf and the subsequent placement of Jennifer in the Special Education Program as a physically handicapped child.

The Child Study Committee had recommended that Jennifer continue her studies in the regular second-grade classroom, the least restrictive environment, with either the teacher or an aide assisting her on and off the toilet at 11:00 a.m. and at

1:00 p.m. When asked to sign a waiver relieving the school of any liability in case Jennifer was injured during this time, Mrs. Godwin refused. She had, she said, reservations about absolving the school of all responsibility. "How do I know," she asked, "somebody won't do something to Jennifer in that situation that would cause her physical or emotional injury?"

Without a waiver, the classroom teacher and the aide had refused to provide the service. Other teachers and aides at the second- and third-grade levels had also refused. "Potty duty isn't part of our job description," the union representative had said.

Because Jennifer's placement in Special Education occurred late in April, the previous principal had resolved the problem temporarily by requesting that Mrs. Godwin come to school twice a day to help Jennifer on and off the toilet. The records noted that if Jennifer still required assistance at the beginning of the next school year, the Child Study Committee recommended placement in the mentally and physically handicapped program located in another part of the building. Two aides for whom bathroom duties were part of the job description staffed the program. Jennifer's parents had voiced strong objections to this recommendation in the spring and indicated they would sue if the district could not provide a suitable academic and physical environment within the regular school program.

Maria laid the file down on her desk. She wondered briefly about the faculty she had not yet met and resisted looking for the names of the teachers who had refused or felt unable to help Jennifer. Realizing she should resolve this issue *before* school started in a few weeks, she decided to walk through the school looking at all of the lavatories in each of the wings. Maybe she would find a more accessible commode. She would also call the director of special education for the school district. She really was not sure what options she had. And she was not sure why the parents had to sign a waiver at all if the conditions for care were stated within Jennifer's Individual Educational Plan (IEP).

Walking through the school, Maria noted that the commodes in the preschool wing were significantly smaller than those in the primary and intermediate wings. She wondered if staff had considered either letting Jennifer use one of these restrooms on her own or installing a smaller commode in the primary or intermediate wing restrooms. Jennifer's file had not included any descriptions of attempts at finding creative solutions to providing a safe and academically stimulating environment. "We have to meet both her physical and academic needs," Maria thought.

A few calls to the district office told Maria that she would not find support for structural changes (such as installation of a smaller commode in the intermediate wing) for the convenience of just one child. She also learned that the district requested that parents sign a waiver when employees were asked to do something outside of their specified job description. Maria decided she should talk with Jennifer's parents to find out how Jennifer was doing.

A few days later, Mrs. Godwin brought Jennifer, now in a wheelchair, to school to meet with Maria. Mrs. Godwin also brought a current medical report. Jennifer had not broken any other bones over the summer, but she still required assistance getting on and off the toilet. Her bone condition had not deteriorated significantly, but the vertebrae were weakening. The doctor believed that Jennifer could continue in a regular school program with minor adjustments in her day. When asked about the reason for Jennifer's wheelchair, Mrs. Godwin explained that Jennifer could walk on her own, but only for short distances. She tired easily. Moreover, getting from the wheelchair to the toilet had exacerbated her original problem.

"But I still won't sign any waiver," Mrs. Godwin explained. "If any harm comes to Jennifer at Bay Elementary, I would not like to have my hands tied." Mrs. Godwin said she would be unable to leave work twice a day as she had in the spring to provide assistance to Jennifer. She would only employ Jennifer's summer babysitter for after school hours once classes resumed. "I'm glad to know," she continued, "that you are working on Jennifer's problems. She is so excited about third grade. She's talked about nothing else all summer."

As Mrs. Godwin and Jennifer left the building, Maria wondered whether schools, even those with well-developed programs in special education, were really prepared to accommodate special children such as Jennifer. She was not even sure what she could do to help.

4.9. Children at Risk

"Tim, what are you doing in the hall again?" asked Doug Faden, exasperated when he saw the lanky sophomore in the hall near the activity wing. "Get back to class."

"I've got a pass, Mr. Faden. I got to take some medicine," Tim responded. "I was hurrying, but I lost my cap."

"You always have an excuse," Faden snapped at him. "Your cap is there, by the water fountain. Now get going."

Moments later the assistant principal responsible for the sophomore class, the science and math departments, the west wing of North Shore High School, and a dozen other areas entered his outer office. His secretary stopped him. "Mr. Faden, Anne Holmes's mother finally telephoned this morning, and her social worker is coming in this afternoon. Also, Ms. Allison dismissed Alan Wakeford from math class because he was disruptive. He's in your office. Finally, Sergeant Kelley at the police department called about Tony Smolett again; they think he might be selling now."

"Thanks. Is there any good news? Never mind, I don't have time for it. How about my meeting with the sophomore counselors at 11:00? Could you check to make sure they are coming? Brenda's having trouble with morning sickness, but I need a report on Tim Wainwright. He was just in the hall again, and I'm losing my patience.

"I'm losing it with you, too, Alan," he said to the boy who was sitting on the green and gold plaid couch inside his office. A huge picture of an eagle, the school mascot, hung above Alan's head. Next to him were several throw pillows in various sizes, with and without additional eagles, all in the school colors. The pillows were gifts from the girl's volleyball team Doug had coached the year before.

"What happened in Ms. Allison's class today?" he asked Alan.

"I'm tryin', Mr. Faden, really I am. I know you're tired of me, but I just can't get math. It's so boring. I forget the rules."

"Okay, detention again. This is your third offense this quarter. The next one is an automatic suspension. Is that what you want?"

"No, but why do I have to take math anyway? I'm not going to need it."

"This is school, remember?" was Doug's retort. "Now it's time for your next class. Hurry and get your books."

Doug picked up the telephone and dialed Anne Holmes's mother. "Mrs. Holmes, this is Mr. Faden at the high school. Anne's test scores came back last week. Anne does qualify for special education assistance, but just barely. I'd hate to see her classified as a special education student when she could perhaps succeed in regular classes."

"I just don't know, Mr. Faden," Mrs. Holmes replied. "I don't have time to work with her at home, and I certainly can't afford a tutor. She isn't getting passing grades now. Can't you just change her to classes that she can pass?"

"Yes, we'll proceed with the special education classification, if that's what you want," he replied, "though I'd really like you to consider other options. I think Anne could succeed with a little help and a little more time and effort."

"I'm sorry, Mr. Faden. I'm doing all that I can."

At 11:00 a.m., Brenda Green and Ken Lefoldt came in together, laughing, for their conference. Brenda dropped her purse beside a chair as she collapsed into it. "I am so happy every day about this time when the morning sickness goes away. Sometimes I think I am allergic to this baby!"

"You had better take care of yourself," Doug replied. "We are going to be so shorthanded while you are on maternity leave that I hate to think about what we'd do if you were gone for any longer than you plan to be."

Brenda looked at him oddly but said nothing. Ken started their weekly session with a question. "Alan Wakeford passed us as we came in. Was he in here again?"

"Yes," Doug responded. "Why is it we're spending all our time with the same kids: Alan Wakeford, Anne Holmes, Tony

Smolett, Tim Wainwright, and five or six others. 'At risk.' Maybe we could at least come up with a new description. The risk is that we'll lose the others because we're spending all our time on so few."

By the time the meeting ended at noon, Brenda felt ravenous, but she asked to speak with Doug for a few minutes alone. "I think you're working too hard, Doug."

"What do you mean?"

"You sound like you're wearing down. I never expected you to worry more about whether the work will get done when I'm gone than you do about whether I'm healthy and my child is healthy."

"I didn't say that, Brenda, and I didn't mean to imply it."

"I know you didn't exactly say that, but you sound as if things are getting you down. Maybe we need to force ourselves to talk about 10 kids each week who have no serious problems, kids who are really doing pretty well."

"Sure," Doug replied, "and that would mean our meetings would be even longer and we'd get even farther behind."

"Listen to yourself. You haven't even finished your second year on the job. How are you going to maintain your energy and your enthusiasm through this year and into the next?"

"Good question, Brenda, and right now I don't have an answer. You think I'll find one on cafeteria duty this noon?"

"Seriously, Doug, think about it. You've got to find some joy in your work. All of us need that. Come on, I'll race you to the cafeteria. This baby is growing on taco salads and ice cream sandwiches."

4.10. Taking a Stand

Elli Javel sat on the wall of the flower garden outside her office and thought about her predecessor, Olivia Perkins. Dr. Perkins had retired the previous spring as principal of Jefferson High School. The garden, established to recognize Dr. Perkins's 30 years of service to the school district, was maintained through the efforts of the Jefferson Parent-Teacher Association. Dr. Perkins had left her mark everywhere in the school. Faculty and staff still frequently referred to Dr. Perkins's sayings, concerns, and interests.

The spirit of Dr. Perkins had become one of Elli's problems. As the newest member of the staff, she dealt daily with people who expected her to respond and manage in exactly the same manner as her predecessor. Having recently graduated from an outstanding doctoral program, Elli had many ideas for instructional improvement that she wanted to implement. She was not willing to let school programs go on as they always had, but she was not sure that she would find much support for change in a faculty that seemed very comfortable exactly as they were.

A few minutes earlier, Mrs. Ballard, the parent of a sophomore student, had left Dr. Javel's office after a conference with Elli. During the conference, Mrs. Ballard had described her 2-year attempt to have her daughter transferred into honors classes. "I honestly dislike 'pushy' parents," Mrs. Ballard had said, "but my child is not challenged. When we moved here 3 years ago, the guidance counselor at the junior high recommended that Megan take regular classes because she needed time to adjust to a new school. Since then I have been unable to find support for having her schedule changed to honors classes. Megan's grades are quite good, and she frequently complains about boredom. Somehow she has gotten lost in the system. For some reason, I have found the English teachers particularly unresponsive, and Megan needs their recommendation to be placed in honors."

Elli was not surprised. Mrs. Ballard was the fourth parent with a similar story she had talked with since school began. Several of the academic departments, but particularly the English department, seemed to include strong departmental chairs who were exclusive rather than inclusive in their approach to serving students. Officially, Jefferson High School did not use tracking, although Elli knew that the levels of courses offered resulted in the same effect. Little movement seemed to occur among the unofficial academic levels, and good students seemed to have little extrinsic motivation to achieve because teachers rarely advanced them to more challenging classes.

To confront this issue, Elli invited Alexis Sutherland, chair of the English department, to stop by for a visit. A tall, slender, impeccably dressed woman with the slightest English accent, Alexis had earned a master's degree in English from the University of Virginia. She often spent part of each summer in Great Britain with relatives. Her classroom walls were covered with posters from the many plays she had seen in London and New York, and her lectures were a delightful mixture of dry British wit and stories of the Romantic poets, the subject of her thesis. Given Alexis's formidable personality, Elli was surprised that the parents she had talked to were not more intimidated.

"Alexis, thank you for taking the time to talk with me," Dr. Javel said as Alexis entered her office a few days later. "In the weeks to come, I hope to meet with each department chair individually, and then all department members as a group, so that I understand each department's philosophy, policies, and operating procedures. The English department seems exceptionally strong. Is my assessment correct?"

As Ms. Sutherland began to reply, much of her formality dissipated, and Elli began to sense a sincere warmth she had not perceived in previous meetings with others present. Alexis mentioned Dr. Olivia Perkins' name often, and Elli reminded herself that change is never easy.

At last, Elli brought the discussion around to policies for placement in honors classes, and Alexis explained, "You know the state has regulations about class size, and once the class sizes are set, it is quite a lengthy process for the guidance counselors to make changes. This has been problematic for the past several years, but it has seemed even more difficult recently as the counselors have been given more responsibilities. I've told the other teachers—that is, we have agreed—that it is best not to recommend anyone for honors classes after registration in the spring for the following year. This policy may exclude some qualified students; I don't know. Our honors program is designed for very high achievers. Nearly everyone from Jefferson who takes the Advanced Placement examination gets college credit."

Elli suspected that state regulations and the success of students on the examination were not the whole explanation. She probed a little further. "What are your thoughts about heterogeneous groupings for classes?"

"I think that would be a dreadful mistake," Alexis replied. "Many of our students come from prominent families. It's amazing, if you think about it, that they have enrolled their children in the public schools when they can afford other options. Those parents would be very upset about mixing their children with, well, underachievers."

After a few pleasantries, Dr. Javel thanked Ms. Sutherland for her thoughts and suggested that they stay in close contact. As she returned to her desk, she considered Megan Ballard and the other students denied placement in Honors English classes. Were they underachievers? Were they simply lost in the system, or had they somehow failed to meet Alexis Sutherland's social criteria for placement? She wondered what Alexis was really saying.

She knew peers and parents recognized Alexis as an exceptional teacher, but she also knew that she could not ignore the issue. Labeling and categorizing children ran counter to everything she believed. She would eventually have to take a stand. She wondered whether the retired Dr. Perkins had ever considered the same questions.

Reflections on Issues of Equity: Questions and Considerations

As noted in the introduction to this chapter, issues of equity are particularly troubling to school administrators. The cases in this chapter raise questions about fairness and about the abilities of organizations to redress social wrongs and to serve individuals well. Use the questions and considerations that follow as beginning points for discussion of equity. Be particularly sensitive to differing perspectives included in these cases and to the differing assumptions that readers bring to the analysis of them. Be wary, knowing that because we live and work in traditional organizations we are often unaware of our biases.

Teachers and discussion leaders may find that groups react strongly when issues of inequality are raised. A recent article in *Teaching Sociology* described three possible kinds of group reactions: resistance, paralysis, and rage (Davis, 1992). The author suggested several ways that groups may be helped to acknowledge inequities without being paralyzed by them and to use their anger to effect changes in the structures that create inequities.

Case 4.1. Equity, Access, and Assessment

1. Elaine Ellender and Superintendent Howard have different assumptions about what is fair in administrative appointments. Contrast their points of view. Which can you more easily support? Which is more valid in this case? Support your responses.
2. Should Darryl Hill be given special consideration for the principalship at Ferndale High? If so, what reasons would you give to Superintendent Howard to support special consideration? If not, why not?
3. Should incumbent position holders, such as Elaine Ellender, influence the selection of their successors? What are the arguments in favor of and against their having influence on selection? Should Elaine have gone to such lengths to support Darryl without preparing him for rejection?
4. Darryl Hill entered the assessment with a preconceived negative opinion of testing. Yet testing is used at all levels of education for many reasons. What could Darryl have done to prepare himself better for both the testing and the position?
5. Did Darryl Hill compromise his principles when he agreed to be tested through the Leadership Assessment Center?
6. Who controls policies for administrator selection in your state and in your district? Who should control such policies? Support your response.
7. Consider the literature on assessment centers and standardized testing. To what degree are assessment centers and

standardized tests biased? Regardless of bias, are they still fairer than other means of selection? Debate whether minority groups achieve greater access or are denied access through standardized testing procedures. For related information, see Bracey (1993), Hambleton (1993), McCleary and Ogawa (1989), Miklos (1988), Phillips (1993), Williams and Pantili (1992), and Witters-Churchill and Erlandson (1990).
8. Consider the literature on administrative succession, especially as it relates to the issues raised in this case. See, for example, Fauske (1987), Firestone (1990), Hart (1988, 1993), Miskel and Cosgrove (1985), and Ogawa (1991).

Case 4.2. Peabody's Blue-Ribbon Task Force

1. What advice would you give to Marge Powers? How can she make the superintendent's wishes known to Mike Rayner and the members of the committee without offending them?
2. Marge tried to anticipate parent concerns in her letter describing trends in grading. Had she talked to you before she sent out this letter, what would you have advised? Was Marge's decision to write the letter appropriate?
3. Marge appointed Mike Rayner to the Peabody Blue-Ribbon Task Force on Quality Education and named him chair. Were these good decisions?
4. The case does not include information about the charge that Marge Powers provided for the Peabody Blue-Ribbon Task Force on Quality Education. What directions should she have provided for the task force?
5. Superintendent Haller is concerned that the task force report will be divisive. Are his concerns legitimate? Should divisiveness always be avoided?
6. Leaders who reject the work of a committee do so at some risk. What could Marge Powers have done to secure the support of Superintendent Haller? What could Superintendent Haller have done to help Marge and the committee?
7. Should data regarding academic achievement, attendance, and disciplinary action be reported separately by gender

and for different racial and ethnic groups? Support your answer.
8. Consider the efforts of school districts to provide equitable education to minority groups. Busing, school pairing, and magnet programs are some of the mechanisms school districts have used. Investigate whether these mechanisms have been effective in providing educational opportunity to minority groups both nationally and in your district.

Case 4.3. But What About Cultural Diversity?

1. Should Ann continue with her plans for a multicultural festival? If you believe she should continue, prepare a plan of action for her. Who should she involve in her plans? Has she learned enough about Rockville to be innovative? If you believe she should abandon her plans at this time, develop an argument supporting your position.
2. Ann considered going around Pritchard and talking to central office staff. Would you recommend she do that?
3. Ann may have taken the position as assistant principal at Rockville without knowing much about the community, the principal, or the responsibilities of the position. What questions might she have asked or what observations might she have made prior to taking the job?
4. What responsibilities are typically given to assistant principals? Refer to the literature on the assistant principalship for additional information, for example, Greenfield (1985), Marshall (1985, 1992a), and Marshall and Mitchell (1990).
5. Consider how the school curriculum might reflect or fail to reflect cultural diversity. Examine the curriculum in history, social studies, English, or science at the high school, junior high school, middle school, or elementary school level for evidence of cultural diversity. Should schools that serve diverse communities and schools that serve homogeneous communities both have curricula that reflect cultural diversity? What kinds of cultural diversity are relevant? For additional information, see, for example, Beane (1990), Grant and Sleeter (1986), and Sleeter (1991).

Case 4.4. "Sticks and Stones May Break My Bones and Names Can Really Hurt Me"

1. How should minority administrators respond to accusations that they have forgotten their own people? Can these accusations just be ignored?
2. Was Doc Berger's advice appropriate? Support your response.
3. Is Mike oversensitive and creating a problem out of nothing? Support your response.
4. As a minority principal, does Mike have more responsibility to meet the needs of the minority community in his school than a White principal would have?
5. Do most principals feel isolated in their work, as Mike seems to feel? Examine studies of the school principalship to test the validity of your answer. See, for example, work by Barth (1990), Cuban (1988), English and Hill (1990), and Wolcott (1973).
6. Consider the difficulties confronted by members of minority groups who seek success in a majority culture. Several studies are relevant to consideration of this issue. See, for example, Bullivant (1987); Heath and McLaughlin (1993); James and Khoo (1991); Marshall (1992c, 1993a); McKenna and Ortiz (1988); Ogbu (1992); Ortiz (1982); Ortiz and Marshall (1988); Rutter, Maughan, Mortimore, Outson, and Smith (1979); Shakeshaft (1989); Valverde and Brown (1988); and Weis and Fine (1993).

Case 4.5. Strength to Do the Job

1. If you were Steve's friend, would you advise him to apply for reassignment? Explain your response.
2. Were the school district's actions in regard to Steve legal, given the provisions of the Americans With Disabilities Act of 1990 (ADA)? Review the major provisions of this act and their applications to people with AIDS.
3. Should Steve, Darla, and the superintendent have been honest with parents and students about the nature of Steve's illness? Support your response.

Equity Issues in School Leadership 97

4. Do you consider Dr. Conrad's response to the member of the local media appropriate? Explain your answer.
5. What support can and should school districts give to a principal who has a debilitating illness?
6. Trace the policies supporting leaves for special nonwork situations such as military service, childbearing, and illness and compare them with the emerging policies regarding people with AIDS.
7. Consider the dilemmas faced by gay and lesbian teachers and administrators. How open can and should gay and lesbian educators be about their sexual orientation? Several studies regarding the challenges and difficulties faced by gay and lesbian educators have recently been published. See, for example, Khayatt (1992), Klein (1992), and Sears (1991).

Case 4.6. Trusting the Institution

1. Should Jack seek a position elsewhere? What advice would you give him about his career?
2. Was it wrong of Jack to assume that the superintendent could commit the school district to Jack's resumption of the principalship at DuPree when he returned from his leave of absence? Are the decisions of individual administrators always subject to change?
3. Was Jack's anger justified when Manning refused to remove Hawkins from the principalship? Were his expectations realistic?
4. Jack is an African-American male. Is that relevant to any of the actions described in this case? Consult the review of leadership development among racial and ethnic minorities by Valverde and Brown (1988), published in the *Handbook of Research on Educational Administration*.
5. How much should one's need for a personal relationship affect career choices and compromises? What are the hazards and risks embedded in each answer to this question?
6. Consider the leave and sabbatical policies of school districts in your area. Are leaves and sabbaticals available to teachers? To administrators? What are the conditions for obtaining

leaves and sabbaticals? What arguments can be made to support the providing of leaves and sabbaticals to certified staff?

Case 4.7. The Humor of *The Hambone*

1. This case ended with several important questions. Can you answer them?
2. Imagine a meeting between Lynelle and the 20 minority students who have threatened to boycott graduation if Bruce speaks as class valedictorian. What issues are likely to be raised? What responses should Lynelle make? What compromises can she suggest?
3. Should Lynelle have acted differently when the first issue of *The Hambone* was published? Was it relevant that no students or parents and only one teacher had complained about that issue?
4. What should Lynelle have done when she realized Bruce had misunderstood her comments?
5. What kinds of help might the superintendent of schools have provided to Lynelle? To what degree is he responsible for the problems with graduation?
6. Consider students' rights of free speech in both school-sponsored and underground newspapers. What court decisions are particularly relevant to this case? What constraints have courts been willing to impose on students' freedom of speech? What position should administrators take when the rights of free speech conflict with legitimate concerns about culture and community in organizations?

Case 4.8. Potty Duty

1. Suggest some options for Maria. What accommodations can be made for Jennifer's disability?
2. Maria spent some of her first weeks in her new position searching for ways to accommodate the special needs of one child. Under what conditions is it appropriate for an administrator to exert a large effort on behalf of a single child? Is Maria acting appropriately here? Why or why not?

3. What options are open to Mrs. Godwin if she disagrees with the Individual Educational Plan proposed by the school district?
4. What help should Maria have reasonably expected from staff in the district office?
5. Review the provisions of the Americans With Disabilities Act (see Case 4.5) and the Individuals With Disabilities Education Act (IDEA) of 1990. First and Curcio (1993) identified a two-part test used by some courts to determine IDEA compliance:
    a. Is education in the regular classroom, with supplementary aids and services, satisfactorily achievable?
    b. If the answer to Part 1 is no, has the school mainstreamed the child to the maximum extent possible? (p. 18)

    Were the school district's actions in regard to Jennifer's placement in second grade appropriate, given the provisions of the ADA and the IDEA? Which of the options suggested in response to Question 1 would be appropriate under the provisions of these acts?
6. The IDEA does not require school districts to provide medical services to children with disabilities. First and Curcio (1993) suggested three questions that school districts might use to determine whether a particular service is medical and thus not required, or related and thus required:
    a. Is the child disabled so as to require special education and related services?
    b. Is the service necessary for the child to benefit from special education?
    c. Can the service be provided by someone other than a physician? (p. 20)

    Using this test, would assistance with using the toilet most likely qualify as a medical or a related service? The following court decisions are relevant: *Irving Independent School District v. Tatro* (1982) and *Detzel v. Board of Education of the Auburn Enlarged City School District* (1987).

7. Consider the tension in the IDEA between the requirement that appropriate educational services be provided and the requirement that children with disabilities be educated with children without disabilities "to the maximum extent possible." Interview school administrators regarding circumstances in which these two requirements may be in conflict.

Case 4.9. Children at Risk

1. Is Brenda right to be concerned about Doug and his attitudes about his work?
2. Is detention an effective means of disciplining a student, such as Alan Wakeford, who finds school boring? Support your answer. What alternatives to detention can you suggest?
3. What is your reaction to Brenda's suggestion that each time they meet, she, Ken, and Doug discuss 10 students who have no serious problems?
4. Doug often uses irony and sarcasm in his reactions to others. Describe how this provides a functional defense mechanism. What might be dysfunctional about the use of irony and sarcasm?
5. Doug spends his time dealing with crises. How might he avoid this administrative trap?
6. Consider how assistant principals, who generally spend much of their time with children who are disruptive or in trouble, maintain a balanced view and sustain energy and enthusiasm in their work. Examine the literature on the assistant principalship (e.g., Greenfield, 1985; Marshall, 1985, 1992a, 1992b, 1993b; Marshall & Mitchell, 1991) and interview practicing administrators to respond to this question.
7. Consider how students who are disaffiliated or otherwise "at risk" can be provided with educational opportunity. Think creatively about alternative school structures and roles for educators that would more effectively address the needs of students at risk. Consult sources on at-risk students such as Fine (1991), Weis (1988), and Weis and Fine (1993).

Case 4.10. Taking a Stand

1. Develop a plan for Elli regarding her work with the faculty on tracking. How can she communicate her ideas to the staff? How will she respond to those who disagree with her? What can and should she do if the majority of the staff disagree with her?
2. How can Elli distinguish herself from Olivia Perkins without offending members of the staff? Could an association with Olivia Perkins be used to her advantage? As in Case 4.1, the literature on leader succession may be relevant.
3. What structural arrangements might Elli use to work with the department chairs?
4. Are teachers more likely to resist change when a new leader is promoting the change?
5. Consider the possible inequities in tracking systems in schools and the arguments given in support of tracking. Who benefits from tracking? What groups have supported policies for tracking, and what groups have opposed such policies? What are the various ways besides achievement in which schools track children? Consult the literature on school tracking. See, for example, Finley (1984), Oakes (1985), Page (1991), and Rosenbaum (1976). Develop an argument in support of, or in opposition to, tracking in secondary schools.

5

Endurance in School Leadership

The cases in this chapter raise several issues related to endurance in school leadership. Those who endure in administrative positions must learn to cope with ambiguity and conflict, make decisions despite the lack of sufficient information and good choices, and protect themselves and their families from the demands of the work. Some writers about leadership (e.g., Bailey, 1988) argue that the very nature of administration taints those who assume administrative roles. Others (e.g., Hodgkinson, 1991; Sergiovanni, 1992; Strike, Haller, & Soltis, 1988) argue that administrators can choose morally defensible approaches to their work. The cases in this chapter challenge readers to define their own moral values and mechanisms for enduring in school administration.

Case Studies of Endurance in School Leadership

5.1. Are Success and Family Like Oil and Water?

He seldom had time for golf, but when the invitation came from the superintendent, he carved out a piece of the afternoon. Whether golf, extra committee assignments, or conferences, Harry Nasaf knew inclusion in "inner-circle" activities was an indication of sponsorship. After 2 successful years as a junior high school principal, he had to make some serious decisions about his aspirations and his future.

On the surface, Harry's life appeared calm. At home, conditions were anything but calm. He knew Darlene was correct when she said, "It's my turn now." As Darlene talked of applying to law school, Harry understood that she would expect him to take over more responsibilities at home. During their 18 years of marriage, Darlene had taken on all the major responsibilities of child rearing. She had been patient, supportive, flexible, and tolerant as Harry wended his way through his teaching and assistant principalship trials. Darlene's reward for her patience and support had been promotion to the new status and unpaid responsibilities of the gracious wife of the principal. Although his countless evenings away from home to supervise sports events and dances, attend school board and committee meetings, and maintain visibility in the community had annoyed Darlene, she had remained good-natured. She knew that he, too, disliked having to assist with the high school football program and thus miss most of his son's fairly spectacular quarterback play in the neighboring school district.

When Harry, with the superintendent's urging, entered the doctoral program in educational administration, he added classes, long hours of reading, and weekends in the library to his routine. Darlene's tolerance had weakened. Their youngest child was entering her teens as a fiercely independent child with an active social life. Darlene, who was about to turn 40, was clearly ready to make some changes in her own life.

Two years ago, when he had come home bursting with news of his principal appointment, Darlene was angry, not elated. His promotion had brought on a wrenching series of heart-to-heart discussions about priorities, health, caring, and fairness. He could still hear the words that hurt most. Darlene had screamed through her tears, "I go to the theater alone. I go to the kids' games and recitals alone. For that matter, I go to bed alone, more often than not."

That night, she had shocked Harry into recognizing the depth of her caring, her needs, her loneliness, and her resentment.

He had always assumed that everyone in the family shared his successes that brought status and pay and benefited the whole family. Harry had pleaded with Darlene to give it a chance, had tried to convince her that he could not possibly turn down this job. He assured Darlene that it was an important stepping stone. It would soon lead to promotion to central office, maybe an assistant superintendency. He had boldly asserted, "I'll be in line for a superintendency in 5 years."

"Maybe," Darlene had replied quietly and sadly, "but will we still be married?"

They remained married, but with sacrifice and compromise. A 6-week vacation in France had improved their marriage. Some personal counseling, which helped Darlene to understand her need to use her own talents, had led to her recent talk of entering law school. Meanwhile, he had jeopardized his doctoral program: incomplete grades in four courses, a "C" in a statistics course, and no clue about his dissertation topic.

He had no plan for salvaging the mess. Harry was no longer the superintendent's only protégé. Three other, younger men in the district were improving their golf games and career prospects, thanks to frequent interaction with the superintendent. Resolving his dilemma was not as simple as choosing between Darlene and the superintendency, but Harry had to make some smaller and interim decisions.

5.2. Does the Job Require Too Much?

Daniel Stipon had been principal of Adrian High School for only 18 months, but he had become the senior administrator in the district at the building level. Seven of the 11 principals had resigned during the past 3 years, and meetings of parents and teachers frequently included references to the decline in morale of teachers and a general lack of school support from parents and other community members.

Daniel could understand the frustrations from both sides. A personable, energetic man in his late forties, he had worked to bring about curricular and instructional changes during the 8 years he spent as an assistant principal in the district. Most of the 1,800 students at Adrian High and their families liked and respected him. Most students and their parents recognized him easily because he attended nearly every after-school event—football games, basketball games, wrestling matches, plays, concerts, anything that involved Adrian students—and because he drove a 1960 Corvette, a car that was aging better than he was.

Spring had been exceptionally beautiful in the Midwest, but the abundance of pollen aggravated Daniel's allergies, and he suffered from a series of sinus infections that forced him to see his physician. Dr. Erickson asked him about his workload. "Oh, about the same as always, only every year there seem to be more meetings."

"What about exercise?"

"Oh, not much lately. I jog a little when I can, and I mow the lawn. Sometimes I think about getting back on the golf course, but I just haven't had time."

"And are you eating properly?"

"Doc, you know the old stereotypes about bachelors. I usually eat something in the cafeteria at noon and stop for something quick on my way home after work. Of course, that's if I don't have an evening obligation."

Dr. Erickson was blunt. He pointed out that 12- and 16-hour workdays in a stressful job would tire anyone, particularly an aging male who used mowing the lawn on the weekends as an excuse for exercise. "You'll have to learn how to delegate," the doctor said. "Didn't you always tell me that's what assistant principals are for?"

"Sure, Doc," Daniel replied, "but I didn't really understand how much Dick Hanson did himself. Now that I'm the principal, everybody expects me to be there for everything. I hate to disappoint the kids."

The following week was a difficult time to start delegating. Spring carnival, a 2-day project for the Parent-Teacher Association, raised over $50,000 for extras such as computers and laboratory equipment. He spent most of the weekend at the event. That week the drama department's production of *Oklahoma* began. Several universities were wooing the lead actress, Elaine Jackson, because of her unusual voice and talent. Persons attending the performance required Daniel's hospitality, not only on Elaine's behalf but also on behalf of other students in future years.

By Sunday night Daniel could hardly breathe. Dr. Erickson explained that the allergies had escalated to near-asthma and threatened to put Daniel in the hospital. "What is it going to take to slow you down?" the doctor asked. "You need to take care of yourself, or you will have no energy to take care of anyone else."

Daniel spent a day in bed taking stock. He worked three or four nights a week going to school activities and community events. He arrived at work by 6:30 a.m. and rarely got home before 8:00 p.m. His marriage had broken up several years earlier, and his relationship with his own children had deteriorated. He had always put a great deal into his work, and as he had done that, the other people in his life had gradually drifted away and found other companions. His limited social life consisted of occasional dinners with old friends who seemed able to forgive him for frequently canceling out at the last minute. Even they had long since given up asking him to play golf or to do anything that required an advance commitment.

Dick Hanson, always a private person, had never really talked with Daniel about the pressure on a principal to support the school at every possible event, to be there in case some kind of trouble occurred, to avoid the whispered questions such as "Why isn't he here?" and "Doesn't he care?" But Daniel knew that Dick had felt the pressures. In fact, Daniel had watched him age in the 3 years he had worked with Dick, and he knew that Dick's wife Mary was eager to have him retire so that they could travel and enjoy life in ways that were impossible when Dick was principal. He also knew that Mary secretly worried that Dick would have a heart attack before he could retire, and they would never have the good times they had postponed for so many years.

Well, he did not know how to do the job any differently. He could delegate responsibilities, but people still expected to see the principal, even if the assistant principal were present or able to handle the problem. Convinced he could not or would not change, he went back to work the next day and by the end of the week submitted his letter of resignation to Karen Moore, district superintendent.

As soon as she received the letter, Dr. Moore telephoned to ask him to meet with her. They talked for 2 hours about the frustrations and stresses of the principal's position. Dr. Moore asked whether Daniel relied enough on his assistants and on senior faculty. When he described what each of the assistants did and the assignments that faculty had assumed in the last year, she seemed satisfied that he was not trying to do everything himself. Still, she seemed convinced that he could delegate more, set priorities, and keep himself healthy by taking some time for himself. "You may have to tell people," Dr. Moore said, "that you can't do everything. You may have to be clearer with the assistant principals and with the faculty about what you can do and what responsibilities will fall to them. We've lost too many good administrators in this district recently, and we can't afford to lose you."

Daniel agreed that Dr. Moore could hold his letter of resignation until he had more time to reconsider. He was not sure, however, that he would ever be satisfied with doing less than he thought the job required. How was one ever to know what was good enough in a job that asked more than any single person could provide?

5.3. Answering the Call

Walking alone on a deserted beach, Donald Warren weighed his options in the late-afternoon sunlight. As an African American who had served as principal at two predominantly minority high schools, he found the offer of the principalship at East Coast High School very tempting. The former principal, Joyce Morrison, had encouraged him to apply, even though Ocean County School District had never hired a Black principal for a predominantly White school. He and Joyce had agreed that the district had to place principals without regard to race. "Besides," Joyce had told him, "you are neither a Tom nor a radical. You say the same thing to everyone, and you stand up for what is right. You're exactly what East Coast High School needs."

With Joyce's encouragement, he had applied for the principalship at East Coast and taken the job when it was offered to him. Now, 2½ half years later, he felt pride in the work he and his staff had accomplished. He had made commitments to the program at East Coast. He had been able to work with the staff to develop the magnet programs in communications and technology. He had successfully courted local businesses and developed strong business partnerships. He had built relationships with the parents and the local school community. He had worked with the faculty and the community to develop a vision that they had not yet fully implemented. Together, they were on the verge of moving to something really outstanding, a school that would attract minority and nonminority students from across the school district. It was a collective vision, not his own Mt. Sinai.

Maybe that was why his conversation with Superintendent George Paxton that morning had left him disconcerted and vaguely disappointed. George had said all the right things. He was asking Don, he had said, to assume the principalship at Jefferson Country Day School, the district's showcase high school. Don was the right person for the job, Paxton had said, because he could do what the superintendent wanted done at Jefferson.

Don asked if he could think about it. The superintendent agreed to give him until the end of the week. Don was not sure what he wanted to think about. The superintendent had offered him a job that most principals only dreamed about. While principals at other schools struggled with order and discipline, the principal at Jefferson could be an instructional leader. Last year, 21 of the school district's 24 National Merit Scholarship semifinalists had attended Jefferson. True, teachers and parents at Jefferson were reputed to be prima donnas, but he was not concerned about his ability to handle them. Rather, he was concerned about the unfinished business at East Coast.

He could turn down the position, he supposed, but he did not think he felt prepared to deal with the consequences. He was not sure what they would be, but he had watched other administrators who had declined to answer the school district's call. Their careers dried up, and they seemed to disappear into the system.

He turned to retrace his steps down the beach. Watching and listening to the surf, walking in the wind were often his way of working through his thoughts. He supposed he had a reputation as a change agent in the district, a person who could go in and clean up. That was not a label he desired. You did not do change and then put it aside. You had to live change, breathe it in, and make it real, he thought. Jefferson would be his third school in 4 years. W. Edwards Deming, his hero, identified "mobility of management" as one of the diseases that stand in the way of real change. He sighed and watched the sandpipers scuttle in front of the incoming waves, wondering what he should do.

5.4. Stretching the Truth

Angela Brown, director of early childhood education programs in the county schools for 5 years, had worked closely with each of the district's eight elementary school principals. She also worked closely with the director of elementary education, and both of them reported to the assistant superintendent of curriculum and instruction. Angela's husband, Moses, was a fourth-grade teacher at one of the local elementary schools, Main Street Elementary.

She had never felt any conflict between her husband's position and hers until now. Last night over dinner, Moses had casually mentioned that his attendance records for his class did not match those kept in the school office. He had been curious about this because the district maintained meticulous attendance records, and he had asked the school secretary how he should go about correcting the mistake. Mrs. Bartholomew had replied, "There's no mistake, Mr. Brown. We're not recording unexcused absences on the official record this year. If we do, we won't meet the criteria for merit pay."

Stunned, Moses had gone directly to Patrick Grady, the principal. "Are we faking the attendance records this year?" Moses had asked.

"Not really," Pat replied. "We're just telling them what they want to hear. Everyone in this school deserves to get the merit bonus, but with the student population we've got, we'll never make the cut. Listen, all of the kids took the standardized tests, but I didn't send all of them in to be machine scored. I kept back the ones that would make us look bad. I scored those myself, and I'll give the results to the teachers and parents. I'll be darned if I'm going to let poor test scores prevent us from getting what we deserve. Come on, Moses, don't look so surprised. Any district that would decide to base teacher and administrator pay on test scores and attendance isn't interested in what kids are really doing. They just want to look good in the newspapers. You know that as well as I do."

Moses had agreed, but now that he knew the school had submitted misleading data, he wanted Angela's approval. "Pat's right," Moses had declared. "We wouldn't be forced into doing this type of thing if the district would just pay us the salary we deserve."

Driving to work the next day, Angela thought about the situation and her concerns. Madison County public schools instituted a merit pay system for administrators and teachers 4 years ago. Having read the research on effective schools, local officials believed that principals play a key role in academic excellence and thus based the annual merit pay on continued increases in test scores, attendance rates, and parent participation. The county commissioners and school board members, all local business people, felt strongly that without this carrot school system administrators would not feel motivated to put forth the extra effort needed to improve school performance. Up until now, Angela had seen merit pay as simply the school system's version of the annual bonus given in the business world. She had never considered that anyone would cheat.

In her professional dealings with Pat Grady, she had developed the highest respect for his work. He cared deeply about students at Main Street Elementary. The demographics of the attendance area for his school had changed gradually over the past several years so that now the school had a higher percentage of minority and poor students than the other district schools. The teachers, however, had maintained good morale and had seemed to meet the challenges head-on. In fact, Angela had spent a great deal of her time at the school because the primary teachers were intensely involved in updating their skills with mathematics and science manipulatives as well as in trying to learn all they could about whole language instruction. Their interest stemmed primarily from their awareness that their students did not learn well from traditional methods. These teachers, Angela thought, did deserve the merit pay bonus if it were based on effort and caring. She wondered whether Pat was justified in altering the records. Another thought occurred to her as she pulled into the parking lot. Moses had not had a merit pay bonus in the past 2 years. She wondered when Pat had begun to fiddle with the test scores. Maybe effort and caring did show up in test scores, but not always at the level needed for the bonus.

Angela went directly to Gerard Franklin's office. Gerard, director of testing and assessment, pulled the second-, third-, fourth-, and fifth-grade test scores for the past 5 years for every district elementary school. The scores from Main Street, however, interested her most. Sure enough, test scores had steadily declined and bottomed out 3 years ago. Third graders at Main Street scored about 2 years below grade level at that time, whereas third graders in the rest of the district had scored at or above grade level. Angela looked at the test scores of the fourth graders for last year. Two years later, fourth graders at Main Street had scored only 1 year below grade level.

The scores for the current year had just come in. Knowing that Pat had selected the tests submitted from Main Street, Angela expected the test scores to be high. They were. They were well above grade level. Angela could not help feeling disappointment that the scores did not reflect the true growth of the children. She was sure that if Pat had not pulled the low tests, the test scores would have shown that the teachers, the students, and the administrators at Main Street were slowly closing the gap. Angela found that possibility much more exciting than the dramatic improvement the bogus test scores indicated. The teachers had worked hard at changing their instructional approaches—that was the real story. The teachers and administrators at Main Street Elementary School were going to be rewarded but for the wrong reasons.

Angela walked back to Gerard's office to return the data sheets. Gerard asked if she had seen anything interesting he could include in his report to the superintendent and the school board. "I'm still mulling it over," she replied. "I might have something to suggest in a few days." Then she returned to her office to wrestle with her conscience.

5.5. Working With Concerned Parents

Phil looked out his office window at his bicycle parked in the rack outside. To just get up, walk out, and go for a quick ride would be simple. Instead of riding away, though, Phil knew he needed to review the Mannette situation. He was not really sure about the wisdom of the decision he had just made. He did know it would keep peace within the school and the teachers' union off his back. It would also mean that one more student would leave Benjamin Franklin Elementary School for a private school.

The problem certainly was not that Franklin needed students. Enrollment was at an all-time high: over 1,400 students in kindergarten through Grade 5. He had even had to turn down an additional kindergarten teacher early in the school year because the school could not accommodate one more class of anything. Phil had not been comfortable making that decision either. In fact, the District Early Childhood Education Committee objected vehemently when Phil had turned down the position. One parent had even called for his resignation. Committee members just had not been realistic or sympathetic to the problems in his school.

Phil had been a teacher in the district for 14 years before becoming an assistant principal. After spending 3 years as an assistant, he now was in his second year as principal of Franklin, the largest elementary school in the city. He knew when he took the position that it would be very demanding. Having two assistant principals helped, but the administrators were still responsible for 8 sections of kindergarten, 10 first grades, 9 second grades, 7 third grades, 8 fourth grades, and 8 fifth grades. The school also housed the district's two classes for trainable mentally retarded children, four preschool sections for handicapped children, and one self-contained section for behaviorally handicapped children. Administrators shared responsibilities equally. Jack, the assistant principal with the most experience, was responsible for Grades 1, 2, and 3. He also handled buildings and grounds. Rose, an older woman with only 2 years of experience as an assistant principal, worked with the kindergartens and all the special programs. Phil was responsible for the rest of the grade levels. He also worked with the parents' advisory groups, community groups, and the school's business partnerships.

Last year, the first grades had been dynamic. Lynne Forte, a teacher transferred from a school across town, had energized almost the entire grade level. No one had complained about the new direction except two teachers who had taught first grade at Benjamin Franklin for over 15 years. Jane and Margaret resented Lynne from the start and resisted anything she suggested. Parents, however, had seemed very supportive of Lynne's efforts. In fact, several had stopped by the school to tell him how much their children's learning and enthusiasm for writing and reading pleased them.

In November or December, Phil had talked to Jack about the changes in the first grade. A few parents had asked about the possibility of having their children moved from Jane's first grade to one of the "creative" classes. As a new principal, Phil had relied on Jack's stock response: "We usually go by the book on these kinds of cases." Should he and Jack have seen this as the beginning of a pattern? Before the year ended, five parents had made similar requests. All had been denied. Three of the five had not enrolled their children for second grade at Franklin.

The Mannettes—he, a doctor; she, a nurse—had only one child in elementary school. Andrew Mannette had done well in Lynne's first-grade class. The Mannettes were so pleased with his progress that they had written a letter to the superintendent praising Lynne's way of working with young children. Still, Phil could not have predicted their negative reaction to Andrew's assignment to Mrs. Whittle's second grade. Phil had not consciously assigned Andrew to any second-grade teacher, but he had noted that Mrs. Whittle was young, vivacious, and pursuing a master's degree at the local university. Surely those ingredients would lead to a creative classroom experience for children. True, he had never observed in Mrs. Whittle's classroom. Besides, second grade should not be a repeat of first grade, and students should learn to adjust to different teaching styles.

The Mannettes felt differently. They wanted Andrew's first-grade experience to continue into second grade. They had even interviewed several of the second-grade teachers and had picked one, Susan Flohr, who talked about "writing and reading workshop," the phrase that Lynne used when she talked about her instructional methods. Mrs. Whittle had told them that she did not believe in the workshop approach and had told them Andrew needed to settle down and learn to do his workbooks quietly. When Phil had talked to Mrs. Whittle yesterday, she had confided that after 1 week of school, she was concerned about Andrew. She might need to refer him for special education evaluation. He seemed to have difficulty concentrating. Lynne apparently had not picked up on that, Phil thought.

So today, in a 90-minute session with Dr. and Mrs. Mannette, he had heard about wonderful Lynne Forte and awful Mrs. Whittle. The Mannettes also told him that other parents intended to demand placement in either Lynne's classroom or in another first grade using the workshop approach. They wanted to know why only one of the second-grade teachers used the workshop approach. They wanted to know whether any teachers in third, fourth, or fifth grade used this approach. Phil told them carefully, and more than once, that individual teachers select their instructional approaches. He said he did not believe in getting involved with instructional methods as long as the methods produced good results.

The Mannettes had then requested that he transfer Andrew out of Mrs. Whittle's classroom and into Mrs. Flohr's class. Phil had stuck with the tradition of not transferring students at a parent's request. With all this uproar in the community over the workshop approach (whatever that was), he felt strongly that parental choice over instructional methods in the classroom could divide his faculty. Neither Mrs. Whittle, nor Jane, nor Margaret was interested in workshops, and he had not seen any in his supervision of the fourth and fifth grades last year. Phil calmly explained his decision to Dr. and Mrs. Mannette. They thanked him for his time, then made an appointment for the next day to withdraw Andrew from Franklin. They informed him they would also write a letter to the superintendent expressing their opinion that Phil should exercise strong leadership on instructional and curricular issues. They would also explain their decision to leave the public school system and tell him that in the future they would encourage other parents to do likewise.

What was he supposed to do? By tradition, teachers select instructional methods; principals make supervision and staffing decisions. However, if he really believed in tradition, why was he not more confident that he had made the right decision for Andrew Mannette?

5.6. How Far Should I Go?

Sitting in his rather dreary office, Paul Green stared at the word *Principal* on the door and thought about Cindi Knight. Paul could remember her staring at him at least a year ago, as she sat alone, tiny and quiet in the lunchroom. When he folded his 6-foot frame to sit and chat with her, she answered no more than a shy "yes" or "no" to his friendly questions. Her face remained blank in response to his attempts at 8-year-old humor. But after that, he frequently saw her around after school. Over time he began to think he had developed a second shadow. Cindi seemed to be there, so he found little errands for her to do, such as carrying stuff to the car or being a messenger for teachers.

When Paul followed up on his curiosity about her, Mrs. Pinkham said of Cindi, "She's a little lost soul; she's in a cloud of daydreams during Reading Circle. But she's no trouble. Thank God, because I have 32 other little terrors and...." Mrs. Pinkham followed with her usual diatribe about kids today and how she *used* to love teaching, her lecture dramatically peppered with examples of the atrocities committed by 8-year-olds and their equally irresponsible parents. Paul got away as soon as he could.

Searching her file later, Paul found nothing extraordinary about Cindi. Her teacher said she was no trouble, so leave it alone, he told himself.

Meanwhile, he needed to spend some time with his own children. When he tried to describe his contacts with Cindi to his wife, she had reacted strongly. "Honey, I know it's your job, but spend some time worrying about Michael's fights." She was right to pull him back to his responsibilities. His three children were no angels. Anyone could see that all Michael needed was for him to spend time doing father-son things to burn off the energy that spilled out inappropriately.

Now, several months later, he had become deeply involved in Cindi Knight's life. He was the first one to notice the bruises. When Mrs. Pinkham confirmed and expanded on the evidence of beatings, he called in Cindi's mother. Regina Knight came in immediately, prepared with a barrage of information and pleas, to convince Paul that the Department of Social Services was handling the problem, that she had kicked out the "SOB ex-boyfriend" who had "done far worse things to me than you've ever seen on Cindi," that she was doing great with a new job and her terrific friends at Alcoholics Anonymous. "Mr. Green, I promise you. I won't ever let Cindi down—I wouldn't let anybody hurt her. I love her so much! You'll see." When Regina left, he had the feeling he had been fooled, but he wanted to believe her.

Some time afterward, Paul managed to shut off his overactive imaginings about Cindi. "I have 288 other kids who need my attention. These days almost every child has some special-needs label or comes from a dysfunctional family." However, Cindi kept quietly shadowing him, reminding him that he had allowed himself to become very involved in her life.

Late one Friday, when every sane and normal administrator and teacher had gone home early, he found his shadow, quietly sobbing on the couch, saying over and over, "Please take me home with you." Apparently, Regina's assurances had, in fact, been a ruse. Cindi was afraid of more beatings from mom if she went home. "Sometimes she sleeps a lot," said Cindi, trying pathetically to say something good about her mom.

Paul knew a weekend with Social Services shuttling her around would be the last thing Cindi needed. He thought, "Tomorrow's Michael's birthday party—there'll be lots of kids and games and a hired clown—maybe it would be great for her—get her mind off her sadness and the kind of pain no little girl should have to face."

He could soft touch his wife into the idea for just the 2 days. He felt so horrible because he knew Cindi's big and ugly new bruises were his fault. He was the guy who had fallen for her mother's story. Now he should rescue his little shadow. Still, a little piece of him said, "No, Paul, don't do this. There's no limit to this. There's only so much you should do. You're going too far; you can't let yourself care this much. It will just cause you no end of trouble."

5.7. Guns Don't Scare Me

The administrators at Westside High School sometimes joked that they had a front line that could beat the Pittsburgh Steelers. Their dimensions were more impressive than those of many college football teams. Jack Mason certainly helped up the averages. He was nearly 6 feet, 6 inches tall and weighed close to 250 pounds, closer than he would like at times. His qualifications for vice principal at Westside included a master's degree and certification in school administration, completion of the course work in his doctoral program, military service, and 6 years of martial arts training. He was not sure which qualifications were more important.

The school district often claimed it carefully matched personnel to positions. At Westside, with a 99% minority student body and a location in a neighborhood with a history of violence, drug use, and drug dealing, the district apparently felt that administrators had to have physical strength and street savvy.

Principal Robert (Bobby) Moore, a minority with deep roots in the neighborhood, understood the students and the community in ways the rest of his administrative team admired. Close to retirement and overweight, Bobbie lacked the physical strength of the rest of the front line. He made up this deficiency in street savvy. His commitment to the education of minority children also earned him the respect of parents and his colleagues in the district.

The dean of boys, Darwin Croft, was White but talked Black. An ex-police officer, he often played the "bad cop" role in the confrontations that he and Jack had with students. "Ladies and gentlemen," Jack would begin in a low, soft voice as he talked to a group of students. That always caught them off-guard and usually got their attention. He would explain the rules clearly and calmly. Then Darwin would step in and repeat the same message in street language laced with threats. In the Black community, the threat often equaled the punishment.

Judith Simmons, the dean of girls, was as tough as the dean of boys in her own way. She was a former physical education teacher and army officer, and she did not back down in confrontations with students.

They were the front line. They had support from the on-duty police officer stationed at the school. A big man himself, he provided support in weapons searches and knife fights. None of the front line was young enough to outrun the students now, but their radios gave them power. They kept in constant contact and could radio ahead the location of a student on the run. The students called them "9" and "Five—0," linking them metaphorically with "9-1-1" and "Hawaii Five—0."

The other women on the administrative staff were isolated from the frequent fights and occasional guns and knives. The assistant principal in charge of curriculum, Marcia Shalley, had participated in the district's weapons search training. She was not physically strong, however, and found the weapons searches unnerving. Marcia took advantage of the district's policy that permitted anyone uncomfortable with weapons searches to opt out. She explained that she lacked the strength to be of any help. The others would end up protecting her, she said, rather than dealing with the guns. Nancy, the second assistant principal and director of the community education program, worked evenings with the assistance of a large minority male.

Friends of his had let Jack know that they thought he was crazy to do this job. "Don't you worry about getting shot?" one woman he dated had asked him. In truth, guns did not scare him. Inner-city kids fought at the least provocation. A simple "he said, she said" exchange could provoke a fight. But the fights ended quickly and rarely involved more than fists and fingernails. However, three guns had been found on the Westside campus in the first 2 months of the school year. Rumors had started one Friday that someone with an Uzi was going to spray the campus to get back at the group of kids involved in dealing drugs. But the truth was that most of the students were afraid of guns and as concerned about safety at the school as the administrators. In fact, administrators had located each of the guns they had found this year because a student had snitched and turned in the report.

His answer to his friend was that most days he did not think about violence at all. He worried about the budget and the staffing changes he had to make because of lower enrollments. He schemed about gimmicks to turn teachers on to the computer technology he loved so much. He spent part of each day handling the flare-ups among students and between teachers and students. He worried about his dissertation proposal and how he was ever going to do the research and keep some balance in his personal life. When the gun reports came in, he did what he had to do. Even the day he took a .357 magnum from a student, he had not really thought about it. His action was, after all, part of the job. If he did not do it, who would?

5.8. The Punk Queen

Lincoln Senior High School, located in a midsize community in the Midwest, prided itself on clean living and upholding traditional American values. The 30,000 residents were mostly Protestant and politically conservative. Because many of the town residents had graduated from Lincoln High, homecoming was a community celebration that included alumni as well as student activities. The crowning of the queen by the mayor during the halftime ceremonies at the football game highlighted the week. For as long as anyone could remember, the queen had been an exemplary member of the senior class. Parents loved to attend the ceremonies and hark back to the good old days when they were young, and they loved to admire the wholesome faces of the queen and her court as well as the athletes. Principal Al Andrews, new to the school and the community just last year, faced a break in tradition.

Su Mallory was spending her senior year with her aunt and was awaiting the birth of her baby in the spring. Su sported multicolored spiked hair, several earrings, and clothing gathered from secondhand shops across the country. She decorated her left cheek with a tattooed butterfly and painted her long fingernails dark purple.

Two weeks before homecoming, Vice Principal Fred Giddings walked into Andrews's office with a stack of ballots in his left hand and announced, "Su Mallory was elected homecoming queen."

Andrews replied, "If this is a joke, it's a bad one. Mayor Housen will have a heart attack on stage." As a member of the Lincoln High School Class of 1964 and president of the Alumni Association, Joe Housen cared about events at the school.

"The vote was nearly two to one," Giddings answered. "Rachel Kleiner was a distant second."

"Rachel Kleiner," moaned Andrews. "An A student, varsity cheerleader, student body president. . . . Do you think the kids like Su that much or that this was a prank?"

"Su has a number of friends, but not this many. Either way, we have a mess," Fred replied. "It would be sad to think that the kids elected someone to make fun of her. I can't imagine Housen fitting the crown over Su's hair spikes."

"What should we do?" Andrews asked. "The kids expect an announcement of the results before the end of the day."

"I think we should announce that Rachel Kleiner was elected queen," Fred answered.

"What did you say?" Andrews responded.

"Announce that Rachel Kleiner was elected," Fred repeated. "Who's to know? Anne McAlister helped me count the votes, but she left school for a doctor's appointment right after we finished. She'll support us. She couldn't believe that Su was elected."

"Let me think about this for a few minutes. Don't mention it to anyone else, and see if you can reach Anne at the doctor's office. Ask her not to say anything either. I just need some time to think."

Fred turned toward the door. "Okay, it's up to you. I'll support you either way. Just let me know what you decide." He left and closed the door quietly behind him, leaving Al to stare out the window in solitude.

5.9. The Retiring Superintendent

Jon Block, principal of Redwoods Elementary School, often thought about the many problems the district faced because of Superintendent Robert Petridge's failure to attend to district needs. No crises had occurred, but in many areas the district lacked genuine leadership. "Petridge used to be a decent administrator," Jon muttered to himself, "before he started thinking about retirement and concentrating on his golf game instead of the problems at hand."

Leigh-Anne Barber seemed to believe that Jon should somehow compensate for Petridge's failures. Leigh-Anne was an ideal teacher. Jon believed that the district should encourage and support strong teachers such as Leigh-Anne. She and her husband Jay lived outside of town in a hillside house built in the early 1920s by an eccentric railroad engineer. Every window provided a spectacular view of the surrounding hills.

Leigh-Anne and Jay loved children. They had two young daughters of their own, and they spent their days coteaching the first grade at Redwoods School. They had 62 students in a large classroom that looked out on the same hills as their home. Within the classroom, however, the Barbers daily faced the same difficulties other teachers of 6-year-olds throughout the state faced. The children were energetic and enthusiastic, but the space was crowded and individual needs often went unmet. Two teaching assistants provided extra adult supervision, but the Barbers had little opportunity to work with the aides and to coordinate the aides' work with their own. These difficulties had been part of the reason for Leigh-Anne's visit.

"It makes no sense that we can't trade in the aides for another full-time teacher," Leigh Anne had lamented to Jon at the end of an especially exhausting day. "Then we would have about 20 students each, and this would be a manageable job. Jay and I could still coteach. In fact, the three of us could coteach some things if we could find a large enough space. Certainly, we could plan together. Can't you talk to the superintendent again?"

"I'll try," Jon had replied, "but you know how things are here, Leigh-Anne. It's only a year-and-a-half now until Mr. Petridge retires, and he isn't interested in anything new. I was very surprised when he agreed to your teaching with your husband. And he has often said that he doesn't think 30 children in a classroom are too many. He remembers the kids around here as they were 25 years ago when he was teaching. He doesn't understand how the area and the children have changed. Just be patient. Things will be different when the new superintendent is appointed."

"I don't think it's fair, Jon, that the children in our care today have to wait for Petridge's retirement. They'll be in third grade by then. This is clearly an inequitable situation. What would you think if Jay and I took our request to the school board? We're famous, you know, since Channel 6 featured us on the news last month," Leigh-Anne concluded with a lilt.

"School board members were pleased by the publicity about our coteaching couple, but that doesn't mean they will accept advice from you or me about how to administer this district in the absence of an active superintendent."

"Maybe you're willing to cool your heels and do nothing for the next 18 months, but I'm not," Leigh-Anne replied. "Come up with something, Jon. You're the one making the big bucks around here!"

5.10. Tragedy

" 'Suicide No Answer,' Students Told" read the headline. The story detailed the reactions to the discovery of Lily Hutchison and Crissy Townsand, dead in an idling car inside a garage in an exclusive subdivision. The suicide note included their apologies for bad grades and disobedience at school. The article continued with quotes from the girls' friends, who said Lily had clashed with her parents because of the four Fs and 17 unexcused absences she had accumulated during the academic term and that she had run away from home recently. Crissy, described as "pretty wild," was often in trouble at school. One friend said Crissy had talked about killing herself but had said it in a joking way so no one took her seriously. The article included warnings from the school psychologist that parents should be alert to possible copycat suicides.

Hal Friendly, principal of the Sewall High School where Lily and Crissy had been 2 of the 1,400 members of the student body, searched through his files and last year's yearbook to piece together his recollections of the two girls; he had to admit he could not remember ever noticing them. The Sewall administrative team division of responsibilities allocated student counseling and discipline to the three assistant principals, and Hal spent most of his time on larger programs and vision building. Demands from new policy directives and district-level meetings consumed his time, especially during the recent campaign for the school building bonds. In fact, his assistant principals ran day-to-day operations.

Hal had to acknowledge that he had been warned that some students were having problems. Brian Davies, a quiet, brainy loner, shot himself last year. After that tragedy, Darwin Coy, the school psychologist, had pleaded for staff development to assist faculty in recognizing potential suicide victims and understanding adolescent development. Hal recalled that plea: "We can't just go on teaching physics and boosting SAT scores as if these kids were robots. Brian came to me about trying to figure out if he was gay! I didn't know how to deal with that, really, and we go on here as if sex and hormones and troubles with self-image aren't happening."

Hal had given the request some thought. In fact, he had talked with two supervisors in central office about developing a grant proposal to support districtwide staff development. But when the push for the bond referendum had begun, the grant proposal had been lost in the confusion. So here he was again, brought up short by his failure to attend to something very important.

Reflections on Issues of Endurance: Questions and Considerations

The questions and considerations that follow emphasize enduring in administration by focusing on the kinds of decisions that administrators must make regarding family, career, and persistent value conflicts. As in the previous chapters, each case could be used to initiate discussion on a number of related issues. In many of the questions, readers are referred to literature in the field. We encourage you to pursue these suggestions. We also indicate that interviews of administrators and teachers may help in discussion of these cases, many of which deal with sensitive issues.

Case 5.1. Are Success and Family Like Oil and Water?

1. Could Harry simply decline the superintendent's invitations to play golf? What risks, if any, would he take in declining these and similar invitations? Are the risks greater, the same, or less than the risks of declining to participate in extra committee assignments or to assist with supervising the high school football program?
2. What personal and professional goals are implied in Harry's actions and decisions? How do these compare with your personal and professional goals?
3. What choices have Harry and Darlene made about division of labor in the family? Does it matter whether these choices have been made deliberately or have evolved without spoken understandings?
4. What advice would you give to Harry about improving his relationships with his family? What advice would you give to Darlene?
5. Are the conflicts between family life and professional life worse for educational administrators than other profession-

Endurance in School Leadership 125

als? Are they worse for women or men? For novice or experienced administrators? What policy changes could ease these dilemmas?

6. Consider the advantages and disadvantages of trying to combine advanced graduate study in a doctoral program with a full-time administrative position. Interview practicing administrators who have completed doctoral programs about the advantages they felt they gained from the degree and the sacrifices they had to make to obtain the degree. Compare the circumstances in this case with those in Case 4.6.

Case 5.2. Does the Job Require Too Much?

1. How important is it that a high school principal be visible at public events? To what degree can responsibilities for these events be delegated?
2. Daniel routinely works 12-hour days. Is that a reasonable job expectation? If so, what qualifications does that suggest for the high school principalship? If not, what is Daniel doing wrong or what might he change?
3. Compare the average number of hours and weeks teachers spend on their work with the average number of hours and weeks administrators in building-level and central office positions spend on their work. What conclusions can you draw?
4. Could a married woman with children be a successful high school principal? Could a single woman or man with children be successful? Support your responses by referring to research on age of career entry and the family and marital status of administrators.
5. Consider the actions that administrators can take to help them handle stress in their jobs. Investigate what the literature recommends. Interview practicing administrators about how they handle job-related stress. Consult studies of life in schools such as those reported in Blase (1991); Cedoline (1982); Cibulka, Reed, and Wong (1992); Gmelch (1993); LeCompte and Dworkin (1991); and Parkay, Currie, and Rhodes (1992).

Case 5.3. Answering the Call

1. Does Donald really have a choice? If he turns down the position at Jefferson, what are the likely consequences?
2. Is it likely that turning down the position at Jefferson would affect his work at East Coast? If so, what influence might it have on his effectiveness at East Coast?
3. Why is "mobility of management" a disease? Investigate what Deming meant and provide examples from school districts and business organizations with which you are familiar.
4. Consider the propensity of school districts to place minority administrators in certain positions. What positions are those likely to be in school districts in your area? What are the staffing patterns in school districts in your region? For additional information, see Acker (1989), McKenna and Ortiz (1988), and Valverde and Brown (1988).

Case 5.4. Stretching the Truth

1. Can equitable merit pay systems be developed for school district employees? Investigate what other school districts have done to develop merit pay systems that have been sustained over a period of more than 3 years.
2. Does the fact that her husband, Moses, is a teacher at Main Street complicate Angela's decision? If so, how is it relevant?
3. Angela wondered whether Pat had been justified in altering the records. Is there any possible justification for what Pat did?
4. What should Angela do? Is the principal really acting unethically? Debate the pros and cons of blowing the whistle about the test scores.
5. Consider the issue of whistle-blowing in organizations. Compare this case to Case 3.2 in chapter 3. The following references on whistle-blowing may be helpful: Glazer and Glazer (1989), Kohn (1988), U.S. Merit Systems Protection Board (1992), and Westman (1991).

Case 5.5. Working With Concerned Parents

1. Should Phil have consulted with the District Early Childhood Education Committee before turning down the additional kindergarten teacher? Why or why not? What other groups might he have consulted with? What arguments would you make supporting or opposing the involvement of each group?
2. How should principals be involved in classroom instructional decisions? Is Phil correct in his assumption that instructional methods are the teachers' responsibility? Explain your response.
3. What support can you provide for the policy against moving children to another teacher's classroom when parents request such a move? What arguments might be advanced against such a policy?
4. Phil appears to assume that Lynne Forte failed to observe that Andrew Mannette was hyperactive. What other possible explanations can you provide?
5. Consider the relationships between the instructional methodologies teachers use and the mission and vision of an elementary school. To what extent can instructional decisions be left to individual teachers and be dependent on the personal preferences of teachers? To what extent should there be schoolwide agreement about instructional practice? Examine the research on teacher work life to illustrate how and to what degree teachers work with each other on instructional issues. Books by Hargreaves (1994), Johnson (1990), Lieberman (1988), Little and McLaughlin (1993), Lortie (1975), McDonald (1992), and Wasley (1991) might be helpful.

Case 5.6. How Far Should I Go?

1. Paul considers taking Cindi into his own home for the weekend. What are Paul's responsibilities? How involved should he get? How would you advise him?
2. Should Paul have investigated Cindi's home situation more? Should he have contacted the appropriate social service

agency when Cindi first appeared with bruises? Investigate the laws in your state that apply in this kind of situation. Would Paul's actions (and lack of action) have been legal in your state?

3. Construct an argument between Paul and his idealistic brother Stephen, a professor of philosophy, about morality and the ethics of caring. For help with positions that could be incorporated into the argument, see Noddings (1992) and Purpel (1988).

4. Consider studies of service professionals such as Lipsky's study of street-level bureaucrats (1980). What mechanisms do those who serve the public use to distance themselves from the problems of those they serve? What are the functional aspects of these mechanisms? What are the dysfunctional aspects?

Case 5.7. Guns Don't Scare Me

1. Describe the matches between the administrators and their positions that are apparent in this case. Is it appropriate for a school district to value physical strength and street savvy in selecting administrators for inner-city schools?

2. Are women disadvantaged in seeking positions in inner-city schools? Are they disadvantaged in seeking assistant principalships?

3. Do you support the school district's policy that those administrators who are uncomfortable with weapons searches can opt out of participating? Argue in support of your position, acknowledging several considerations that support an opposite view.

4. Provide examples of how administrators might use the "good cop, bad cop" approach. You might look for examples in relationships with students, as in this case, and also in relationships with teachers and parents.

5. Jack appears to do his job as assistant principal without considering the personal physical risks involved for himself or for others. In fact, some might call him unreflective, at least about this aspect of his job. Is this a healthy approach? If you were Jack's friend, what advice would you give him?

Endurance in School Leadership

6. Consider the changes in administrative positions, physical facilities, and operating costs in schools related to violence, threats of violence, and concerns about violence in the schools. Examine the measures that school districts have taken to deal with violence. Are any of these measures incongruent with the development of schools as learning communities? What are alternative approaches and different ways of thinking about school violence?

Case 5.8. The Punk Queen

1. What should Al do? Argue in support of your position.
2. Suppose that Al had compelling evidence that Su was elected because several members of the student body thought that would make a good joke. Would that change your decision?
3. Is Fred correct in his assumption that no one will know whether the count is accurate? What consequences are likely if administrators decide to announce Rachel was elected and their ruse is discovered by students?
4. Could an administrator's code of ethics incorporate a justification for keeping the real vote quiet? Explain your response.
5. Consider the extent to which the sponsors of school events such as homecoming celebrations should be responsive to the interests and concerns of community members. Are the possible reactions of the mayor relevant to the decisions that Al and Fred must make?

Case 5.9. The Retiring Superintendent

1. Leigh-Anne believes that Jon is responsible for doing something about what she perceives as an inequitable situation. Do you concur? Support your position.
2. Leigh-Anne has threatened to take her concerns to the school board. If she does take her concerns to the board, what approach should she use? What, if anything, should Jon do?
3. How are conflicts over such issues as the appropriate number of children in a class resolved within school districts? Should such issues be resolved at the school level or the district level? Argue in support of your position.

4. Is there anything that subordinates in an organization can do about a superior who has essentially retired on the job? Jon's position appears to be that nothing can be done. Is this prudent or simply lazy?
5. Consider administrative salary structures within a school district. Who does, in fact, get the "big bucks"? What, if any, additional responsibilities go with those positions? Identify the assumptions that undergird the administrative salary structure. What other assumptions might be as appropriate? How might schools change if teachers, those working closest to the children, got the big bucks?

Case 5.10. Tragedy

1. Is Hal at all responsible for the students' suicides? What actions might he have taken?
2. Administrators are often faced with conflicting priorities and must make choices that they might later wish they could reconsider. What coping mechanism do they use to deal with the consequences of choices they have made? What aspects of these coping mechanisms are functional? What aspects are dysfunctional?
3. What are the responsibilities of schools and school districts to provide assistance to adolescents with psychological problems? Compare and contrast your response to this question to the responses of others. What assumptions about the role of schools in society are implied by the responses you examine?
4. What kinds of special training and what school policies would help administrators deal with these kinds of situations?
5. Consider the similarities between this case and Case 5.6. In both cases children have suffered and administrators might have been able to take action to prevent or minimize the suffering. Are the administrators in these cases equally culpable? Are any of them culpable at all? What moral obligations do administrators have to do all that they can to aid children? How can they be certain that what they have done is enough?

References

Acker, S. (Ed.). (1989). *Teachers, gender and careers*. London: Falmer.
Anderson, G. L., & Page, B. (1993, April). *Narrative knowledge and educational administration: The stories that guide our practice*. Paper presented at the annual meeting of the American Educational Research Association, Atlanta, GA.
Ashbaugh, C. R., & Kasten, K. L. (1991). *Educational leadership: Case studies for reflective practice*. New York: Longman.
Ashbaugh, C. R., & Kasten, K. L. (1992). *The licensure of school administrators: Policy and practice*. Washington, DC: American Association of Colleges for Teacher Education.
Bailey, F. G. (1988). *Humbuggery and manipulation: The art of leadership*. Ithaca, NY: Cornell University Press.
Barth, R. S. (1990). *Improving schools from within: Teachers, parents, and principals can make the difference*. San Francisco: Jossey-Bass.
Beane, J. A. (1990). *Affect in the curriculum: Toward democracy, dignity, and diversity*. New York: Teachers College Press.
Bell, C., & Chase, S. (1993). The underrepresentation of women in school leadership. In C. Marshall (Ed.), *The new politics of race and gender* (pp. 141-154). London: Falmer.
Blase, J. (Ed.). (1991). *The politics of life in schools*. Newbury Park, CA: Sage.
Bourne, P. G., & Winkler, N. J. (1982). Commitment and the cultural mandate: Women in medicine. In R. Kahn-Hut,

A. K. Daniels, & R. Colvard (Eds.), *Women and work: Problems and perspectives* (pp. 11-122). New York: Oxford University Press.

Boyd, W. L. (1983). *Political science and educational administration: Rethinking educational policy and management in the 1980's*. Victoria, Australia: Deakin University Press.

Bracey, G. W. (1993). Assessing the new assessments. *Principal, 72*(3), 34-36.

Bredeson, P. V. (1985). An analysis of the metaphorical perspectives of school principals. *Educational Administration Quarterly, 21*(1), 29-50.

Breer, D., & Locke, B. (1965). *Task experience as a source of attitudes*. Homewood, IL: Dorsey Press.

Brookfield, S. (1992). Uncovering assumptions: The key to reflective practice. *Adult Learning, 3*(4), 13-14, 18.

Bullivant, B. M. (1987). *The ethnic encounter in the secondary school: Ethnocultural reproduction and resistance*. New York: Falmer.

Burks, M. P. (1989). *Requirements for certification for elementary schools, secondary schools, and junior colleges* (53rd ed.). Chicago: University of Chicago Press.

Calabrese, R. (1988). Ethical leadership: A prerequisite for effective schools. *NASSP Bulletin, 72*(512), 1-4.

Callahan, R. E. (1962). *Education and the cult of efficiency: A study of the social forces that have shaped the administration of the public schools*. Chicago: University of Chicago Press.

Cedoline, A. J. (1982). *Job burnout in public education: Symptoms, causes, and survival skills*. New York: Teachers College Press.

Cibulka, J., Reed, R., & Wong, I. (1992). *The politics of urban education in the United States*. London: Falmer.

Clark, D. L., & Astuto, T. A. (1986). The significance and permanence of changes in federal education policy. *Educational Researcher, 15*(8), 3-14.

Cooper, B. S., & Boyd, W. L. (1987). The evolution of training for school administrators. In J. Murphy & P. Hallinger (Eds.), *Approaches to administrative training in education* (pp. 3-21). Albany: SUNY Press.

Cornett, L. (1985). *Rethinking the selection and preparation of school principals*. Paper presented to the National Governors' Association Task Force on School Leadership and Management, Little Rock, AR.

Cuban, L. (1988). *The managerial imperative and the practice of leadership in schools*. Albany: SUNY Press.

Davis, N. J. (1992). Teaching about inequality: Student resistance, paralysis, and rage. *Teaching Sociology, 20*, 232-238.

Detzel v. Board of Education of the Auburn Enlarged City School District, 637 F. Supp. 1022 (N.D.N.Y. 1986), aff'd mem., 820 F.2d 587 (2d Cir.); cert. den., 484 U.S. 981, 108 S.Ct. 495, 98 L.Ed. 3d 494 (1987).

English, F. W., & Hill, J. C. (1990). *Restructuring: The principal and curriculum change*. Reston, VA: National Association of Secondary School Principals.

Evers, C. W., & Lakomski, G. (1991). *Knowing educational administration*. New York: Pergamon.

Fauske, J. R. (1987). Detachment, fear, and expectation: A faculty's response to the impending succession of its principal. *Educational Administration Quarterly, 23*(2), 23-44.

Ferguson, K. E. (1984). *The feminist case against bureaucracy*. Philadelphia: Temple University Press.

Fine, M. (1991). *Framing dropouts: Notes on the politics of an urban public high school*. Albany: SUNY Press.

Finley, M. K. (1984). Teachers and tracking in a comprehensive high school. *Sociology of Education, 57*, 233-243.

Firestone, W. A. (1990). Succession and bureaucracy: Gouldner revisited. *Educational Administration Quarterly, 26*, 345-375.

First, P. F., & Curcio, J. L. (1993). *Individuals with disabilities: Implementing the newest laws*. Newbury Park, CA: Corwin.

Foster, W. (1986). *Paradigms and promises: New approaches to educational administration*. New York: Prometheus.

Foster, W. (1989). Toward a critical practice of educational leadership. In J. Smyth (Ed.), *Critical perspectives on educational leadership* (pp. 39-62). New York: Falmer.

Gaertner, K. N. (1980). The structure of organizational careers. *Sociology of Education, 53*, 7-20.

Giroux, H. A. (1992). Educational leadership and the crisis of democratic government. *Educational Researcher, 21*(4), 4-11.

Glazer, M. P., & Glazer, P. M. (1989). *The whistleblowers: Exposing corruption in government and industry.* New York: Basic Books.

Gmelch, W. H. (1993). *Coping with faculty stress.* Newbury Park, CA: Sage.

Grant, C. A., & Sleeter, C. E. (1986). *After the school bell rings.* Philadelphia: Falmer.

Greenfield, W. (1985). Studies of the assistant principalship: Toward new avenues of inquiry. *Education and Urban Society, 18*(1), 7-23.

Griffiths, D. E. (1979). Intellectual turmoil in educational administration. *Educational Administration Quarterly, 15,* 43-65.

Griffiths, D. E., Goldman, S., & McFarland, W. (1965). Teacher mobility in New York City. *Educational Administration Quarterly, 1,* 15-31.

Hambleton, R. K. (1993). *Advances in the detection of differentially functioning test items.* (ERIC Document Reproduction Service No. ED 356 264)

Hargreaves, A. (1994). *Changing teachers, changing times: Teachers' work and culture in the postmodern age.* New York: Teachers College Press.

Harrington, H. L., & Garrison, J. W. (1992). Cases as shared inquiry: A dialogical model of teacher preparation. *American Educational Research Journal, 29,* 715-735.

Hart, A. W. (1988). Attribution as effect: An outsider principal's succession. *Journal of Educational Administration, 26,* 331-352.

Hart, A. W. (1993). *Principal succession: Establishing leadership in schools.* Albany: SUNY Press.

Heath, S. B., & McLaughlin, M. W. (Eds.). (1993). *Identity and inner-city youth: Beyond ethnicity and gender.* New York: Teachers College Press.

Hodgkinson, C. (1991). *Educational leadership: The moral art.* Albany: SUNY Press.

Inkles, A. (1973). Social structure and socialization. In D. Goslin (Ed.), *Handbook of socialization theory and research* (pp. 615-632). Chicago: Rand McNally.

Irving Independent School District v. Tatro, 468 U.S. 883, 104 S.Ct. 3371, 82 L.Ed.2d 690 (1982).

James, K., & Khoo, G. (1991). Identity-related influences on the success of minority workers in primarily nonminority organizations. *Hispanic Journal of Behavioral Sciences, 13,* 169-192.

Johnson, S. M. (1990). *Teachers at work: Achieving success in our schools.* New York: Basic Books.

Kasten, K., & Ashbaugh, C. R. (1991). The place of values in superintendents' work. *Journal of Educational Administration, 29*(3), 54-66.

Khayatt, M. D. (1992). *Lesbian teachers: An invisible presence.* Albany: SUNY Press.

Kimbrough, R. (1985). *Ethics: A course of study for educational leaders.* Arlington, VA: American Association of School Administrators.

Klein, S. S. (1992). *Sex equity and sexuality in education.* Albany: SUNY Press.

Kohn, S. M. (1988). *The labor lawyer's guide to the rights and responsibilities of employee whistleblowers.* New York: Quorum Books.

LeCompte, M. D., & Dworkin, A. G. (1991). *Giving up on school: Student dropouts and teacher burnouts.* Newbury Park, CA: Corwin.

Leithwood, K. A. (1992). The move toward transformational leadership. *Educational Leadership, 49*(5), 8-12.

Licata, J. W., & Hack, W. G. (1980). School administration grapevine structure. *Educational Administration Quarterly, 16*(3), 82-99.

Lieberman, A. (Ed.). (1988). *Building a professional culture in schools.* New York: Teachers College Press.

Lipsky, M. (1980). *Street-level bureaucracy: Dilemmas of the individual in public services.* New York: Russell Sage.

Little, J. W., & McLaughlin, M. W. (1993). *Teachers' work: Individuals, colleagues, and contexts.* New York: Teachers College Press.

Lortie, D. (1975). *Schoolteacher: A sociological study.* Chicago: University of Chicago Press.

Marshall, C. (1985). Professional shock: The enculturation of the assistant principal. *Education and Urban Society, 18*(1), 28-58.

Marshall, C. (1988). Analyzing the culture of school leadership. *Education and Urban Society, 20*(1), 262-275.

Marshall, C. (1991). Educational policy dilemmas: Can we have control and quality and choice and democracy and equity? In K. Borman, P. Swami, & L. Wagstaff (Eds.), *Contemporary issues in U.S. education* (pp. 1-21). Norwood, NJ: Ablex.

Marshall, C. (1992a). *The assistant principal: Leadership choices and challenges.* Newbury Park, CA: Corwin.

Marshall, C. (1992b). School administrators' values: A focus on atypicals. *Educational Administration Quarterly, 28*(3), 368-386.

Marshall, C. (Ed.). (1992c). *Women as school administrators.* Bloomington, IN: Phi Delta Kappa Center for Evaluation, Development, and Research.

Marshall, C. (1993a). The politics of denial: Gender and race issues in administration. In C. Marshall (Ed.), *The new politics of race and gender* (pp. 168-174). London: Falmer.

Marshall, C. (1993b). *The unsung role of the career assistant principal.* Washington, DC: National Association of Secondary School Principals.

Marshall, C., & Mitchell, B. (1990, April). *The assumptive worlds of fledgling administrators.* Paper presented at the annual conference of the American Educational Research Association, Boston, MA.

Marshall, C., Mitchell, D., & Wirt, F. (1989). *Culture and education policy in the American states.* London: Falmer.

Marshall, C., & Mitchell, M. (1991). The assumptive worlds of fledging administrators. *Education and Urban Society, 23*(4), 396-415.

Marshall, C., Rogers, D., & Steele, J. (1993, April). *Caring as career: An alternative model for educational administration.* Paper presented at the annual conference of the American Educational Research Association, Atlanta, GA.

McCleary, L. E., & Ogawa, R. (1989). The assessment center process for selecting school leaders. *School Organization, 9*(1), 103-113.

McDonald, J. P. (1992). *Teaching: Making sense of an uncertain craft.* New York: Teachers College Press.

McGregor, D. M. (1960). *The human side of enterprise.* New York: McGraw-Hill.

McKenna, T., & Ortiz, F. I. (Eds.). (1988). *The broken web: The educational experience of Hispanic American women.* Berkeley, CA: Floricanto.

Merton, R. K. (1964). *Social theory and social structure.* London: Free Press.

Miklos, E. (1988). Administrator selection, career patterns, succession, and socialization. In N. Boyan (Ed.), *The handbook of research in educational administration* (pp. 53-76). White Plains, NY: Longman.

Miskel, C., & Cosgrove, D. (1985). Leader succession in school settings. *Review of Educational Research, 55,* 87-105.

Mitchell, D. (1982, April). *Metaphors of management or how far from outcomes can you get?* Paper presented at the annual meeting of the American Educational Research Association, New York.

National Education Association. (1986). *Conditions and resources of teaching.* Washington, DC: Author.

National Governors' Association. (1991). *Time for results: The governors' 1991 report on education.* Washington, DC: The National Governors' Association Center for Policy Research and Analysis.

Noddings, N. (1992). *The challenge to care in schools: An alternative approach to education.* New York: Teachers College Press.

Oakes, J. (1985). *Keeping track: How schools structure inequality.* New Haven, CT: Hale University Press.

Ogawa, R. T. (1991). Enchantment, disenchantment, and accommodation: How a faculty made sense of the succession of its principal. *Educational Administration Quarterly*, 27(1), 30-60.

Ogbu, J. U. (1992). Understanding cultural diversity and learning. *Educational Researcher*, 21(8), 5-14.

Ortiz, F. I. (1982). *Career patterns in education: Women, men, and minorities in school administration*. South Hadley, MA: J.F. Bergin.

Ortiz, F. I., & Marshall, C. (1988). Women in educational administration. In N. Boyan (Ed.), *The handbook of research in educational administration* (pp. 123-141). New York: Longman.

Osterman, K. R., & Kottkamp, R. B. (1993). *Reflective practice for educators: Improving schooling through professional development*. Newbury Park, CA: Corwin.

Owens, R. G. (1991). *Organizational behavior in education*. Englewood Cliffs, NJ: Prentice-Hall.

Page, R. N. (1991). *Lower-track classrooms: A curricular and cultural perspective*. New York: Teachers College Press.

Parkay, F. W., Currie, G. D., & Rhodes, J. W. (1992). Professional socialization: A longitudinal study of first-time high school principals. *Educational Administration Quarterly*, 28, 43-75.

Pascale, R. T. (1985). The paradox of corporate culture: Reconciling ourselves to socialization. *California Management Review*, 27(2), 26-41.

Phillips, S. E. (1993). Legal issues in performance assessment. *West Education Law Quarterly*, 2, 329-358.

Popkewitz, T. S., Tabachnick, B. R., & Wehlage, G. (1982). *The myth of educational reform: A study of school responses to a program of change*. Madison: University of Wisconsin Press.

Purpel, D. (1988). *The moral and spiritual crisis in education*. Hadley, MA: Bergin & Garvey.

Reitzug, U. C. (1992). Self-managed leadership: An alternative school governance structure. *Urban Review*, 24(2), 133-147.

Rosenbaum, J. E. (1976). *Making inequality: The hidden curriculum of high school tracking*. New York: Wiley.

Rutter, M., Maughan, B., Mortimore, P., Outson, J., & Smith, A. (1979). *Fifteen thousand hours: Secondary schools and their*

effects on children. Cambridge, MA: Harvard University Press.
Schein, E. H. (1986). *Organizational culture and leadership.* San Francisco: Jossey-Bass.
Schön, D. A. (1983). *Educating the reflective practitioner.* San Francisco: Jossey-Bass.
Sears, J. T. (1991). *Growing up gay in the South: Race, gender, and journeys of the spirit.* New York: Harrington Park Press.
Sergiovanni, T. J. (1991). Constructing and changing theories of practice: The key to preparing school administrators. *Urban Review, 23*(1), 39-49.
Sergiovanni, T. J. (1992). *Moral leadership: Getting to the heart of school improvement.* San Francisco: Jossey-Bass.
Sergiovanni, T. J., & Starratt, R. J. (1983). *Supervision: Human perspectives* (3rd ed.). New York: McGraw-Hill.
Shakeshaft, C. (1989). *Women in educational administration.* Newbury Park, CA: Corwin.
Sleeter, C. (Ed.). (1991). *Empowerment through multicultural education.* Albany: SUNY Press.
Starratt, R. J. (1991). Building an ethical school: A theory for practice in educational leadership. *Educational Administration Quarterly, 27*(2), 185-202.
Strike, K. A., Haller, E. J., & Soltis, J. F. (1988). *The ethics of school administration.* New York: Teachers College Press.
Thompson, S. D. (1989). Commentary. In J. Hannaway & R. Crowson (Eds.), *The politics of reforming school administration* (pp. 201-218). London: Falmer.
Turner, R. (1960). Sponsored and contest mobility and the school system. *American Sociological Review, 25,* 855-867.
Tyack, D., & Hansot, E. (1982). *Managers of virtue: Public school leadership in America 1820-1980.* New York: Basic Books.
U.S. Merit Systems Protection Board. (1992). *Questions and answers about whistleblower appeals.* Washington, DC: Author.
Valverde, L. (1974). *Succession socialization: Its influence on school administrative candidates and its implications on the exclusion of minorities from administration.* Washington, DC: National Institute of Education. (ERIC Document Reproduction Service No. ED 093 052)

Valverde, L. A., & Brown, F. (1988). Influences in leadership development among racial and ethnic minorities. In N. Boyan (Ed.), *The handbook of research on educational administration* (pp. 143-158). New York: Longman.

Van Maanan, J., & Schein, E. H. (1979). Toward a theory of organizational socialization. *Research in Organizational Behavior, 1,* 209-264.

Wasley, P. (1991). *Teachers who lead: The rhetoric of reform and the realities of practice.* New York: Teachers College Press.

Weatherly, R., & Lipsky, M. (1977). Street-level bureaucrats and institutional innovation: Implementing special education reform. *Harvard Educational Review, 47*(2), 171-197.

Weis, L. (Ed.). (1988). *Class, race, and gender in American education.* Albany: SUNY Press.

Weis, L., & Fine, M. (Eds.). (1993). *Beyond silenced voices: Class, race, and gender in United States schools.* Albany: SUNY Press.

Westman, D. P. (1991). *Whistleblowing: The law of retaliatory discharge.* Washington, DC: Bureau of National Affairs.

Williams, J., & Pantili, L. (1992). A meta-analytic model of principal assessment. *Journal of School Leadership, 2,* 256-279.

Witters-Churchill, L., & Erlandson, D. A. (Eds.). (1990). *The principalship in the 1990s and beyond: Current research on performance-based preparation and professional development.* Tempe, AZ: University Council on Educational Administration.

Wolcott, H. F. (1973). *The man in the principal's office: An ethnography.* New York: Holt, Rinehart & Winston.

In compliance with GPSR, should you have any concerns about the safety of this product, please advise: International Associates Auditing & Certification Limited The Black Church, St Mary's Place, Dublin 7, D07 P4AX Ireland
EUAR@ie.ia-net.com

www.ingramcontent.com/pod-product-compliance
Lightning Source LLC
Chambersburg PA
CBHW072043290426
44110CB00014B/1566